In this remarkable new book, *The Competitive Edge*, sport psychologist Dr. Jeff Brown helps readers explore their personal values as they are acquired, challenged, and refined over time through sport training and competition experiences. The seven principles he offers and elegantly discusses will be useful to those who seek to learn more about themselves and the game of life. Christians and people across faith orientations will find in this practical, readable book a treasure for now and years to come.

Edward F. Etzel, EdD
Psychologist and Associate professor, West Virginia University

The famous twentieth century journalist Heywood Broun said "Sports do not build character. They reveal it." As a sport psychologist and member of the Boston Marathon Medical Care Team for many years, Jeff Brown helps fallen competitors understand the psychological complexity of winning versus losing. In his remarkable book, *The Competitive Edge*, Brown shows how the important qualities of character and integrity lead to winning not only in sports, but also in achieving life goals. The text is lighthearted, witty, and most importantly, insightful. This book is a winner.

Marvin M. Adner, MD
Medical director, Boston Marathon 1978–2006

Dr. Jeffrey Brown's precise book about integrity and the human spirit is seamlessly universal and inspirational. I highly recommend this enjoyable, yet pensive, book.

J. Michael Moncrief
Actor, *The Legend of Bagger Vance*

The Competitive Edge will help you weed out the things in your life that wear black hats, it will help you eliminate the bad guys, and lead you down many years of Happy Trails. Even if you don't come in first, you're still a winner! I love this book!

Roy Rogers Jr.
President, Roy Rogers–Dale Evans Happy Trails Theater & Museum

This is an important topic that doesn't get discussed enough. In *The Competitive Edge*, Dr. Jeff Brown has nailed it. As Christians, we must have a different playbook. Winning without integrity is not winning. I know of no one better qualified to provide wisdom on this principle than Jeff Brown. I highly recommend this book.

Frank J. Lofaro
President and Chief Operating Officer, Christian Management Association

Your integrity is your most valuable asset in today's global marketplace, not to mention in your own home . . . and the heavenly home that awaits us. In *The Competitive Edge*, Jeff Brown weighs in on the age-old clash between playing to win and playing fair, showing us that it is possible to do both.

Sheila Heen
Coauthor of *Difficult Conversations: How to Discuss What Matters Most*

The Competitive Edge serves up some surprising insights that can benefit everyone from the pro athlete to the weekend warrior, from the exec in the office to the kid in school. A superb book that transcends its sports-based theme to offer valuable keys for living a better life, too.

Jim Vitti
Author of *The Cubs on Catalina, Southern Gold, A Little Piece of Paradise,* and *Publicity Handbook*

As a non-Christian sport psychologist, I approached Jeff Brown's book with some hesitation, wondering how the combination of religious orientation and mental training techniques would work for someone like me. The ultimate irony was that his guide to maintaining integrity and staying in touch with core values became a useful road map for me as I struggled with the very question of how to honestly endorse a book when I could not fully embrace everything it had to say. That being said, I feel entirely comfortable and true in saying that this book will be very useful for both Christians and non-Christians alike. It provides compelling stories and a variety of religiously based and secular strategies for staying true to oneself while engaging fully in the competitive world we live in, be it business or sport.

Kirsten Peterson
Senior sport psychologist, United States Olympic Committee

The Competitive Edge offers a powerful message to those of us who seek athletic success while fulfilling God's will and plan for our life. Jeff Brown offers a seven-principle plan that will enable you to achieve peak performance, fight the good fight, and finish the race.

Ian McCaw
Director of Athletics, Baylor University

Dr. Jeffrey Brown has crafted a great book for all people looking to balance a competitive spirit with moral and personal integrity. Having attempted to do this very thing on CBS's *Survivor*, I am keenly aware of just how difficult a negotiation this balance can be. Life, like *Survivor*, is filled with moments that suggest: "Just this once, it's not a big deal." But in truth, compromising one's values is always a big deal. Thanks to Dr. Brown's book, I am more fully prepared to face these compromising situations with my integrity intact.

Austin Carty
Contestant, *Survivor: Panama–Exile Island*

Dr. Jeff Brown identifies seven principles that are absolute necessities in living a life of character and integrity. Christians do not need to sacrifice their competitiveness to live a believer's life. Jeff Brown has done a superb job of encouraging that competitive nature while drawing closer to Christ.

Ron Wellman
Director of Athletics, Wake Forest University

Through engaging stories and anecdotes, Dr. Jeffrey Brown offers a winning road map for athletes and other competitors. The tools of sport psychology, combined with central awareness of your values, character, and integrity, will give you the competitive edge.

Dr. Kate F. Hays
Past president, Division of Exercise & Sport Psychology, American Psychological Association
Founder and director, Toronto Marathon Psyching Team
Fellow, Association for Applied Sport Psychology
Author, *Move Your Body, Tone Your Mood*

Dr. Brown's principles are like sport psychology parables—inspiring, useful, and a great resource for the integrity-driven, high-performance life.

Carol Kauffman, PhD ABPP
Assistant clinical professor, Harvard Medical School

The Competitive Edge is a must read for anyone who competes, whether in athletics, business, academics, or any other entity. *The Competitive Edge* will have a great impact on the way you view competition in today's world. The principles in this book have changed the way I see competition in our culture.

Rico Petrocelli
President, Petrocelli Marketing Group
Author of *Tales from the Impossible Dream Red Sox*

The Competitive Edge is an incredibly motivating book for anyone striving to succeed in this world. It will change your perspective on what it truly means to win and what each victory should and shouldn't cost. Your integrity and overall character will be challenged for the better as you take in the wisdom and experiences offered to you by author Dr. Jeff Brown.

Joe White
President, Kanakuk Kamps

Jeff Brown's modern-day parables are valuable lessons we can all learn and abide by in the perpetual quest of bettering ourselves. *The Competitive Edge* reminds us that our day-to-day ambitions need to be examined and conform to the proper perspective of our overall lives. I am honored to issue my very own Letter of Authenticity and encourage readers of all faiths to indulge in such a fine compilation.

James Spence Jr.
Autograph expert

THE COMPETITIVE EDGE

THE COMPETITIVE EDGE

HOW TO WIN EVERY TIME YOU COMPETE

DR. JEFFREY BROWN

TYNDALE HOUSE PUBLISHERS, INC.
CAROL STREAM, ILLINOIS

Library of Congress Cataloging-in-Publication Data

Brown, Jeffrey.
    The competitive edge : how to win every time you compete / Jeffrey Brown.
        p. cm.
    ISBN-13: 978-1-4143-1330-6 (hc : alk. paper)
    ISBN-10: 1-4143-1330-6 (hc : alk. paper)
    1. Success—Religious aspects—Christianity. 2. Christian life. 3. Competition.
I. Title.
    BV4598.3.B76 2007
    248.4—dc22   2007018202

Printed in the United States of America.

12   11   10   09   08   07
 7   6   5   4   3   2   1

To my wife, Carolynne,
whose character strengthens mine.

And to my son, Grant,
for whom my own integrity should matter most.

CONTENTS

ACKNOWLEDGMENTS

Getting a book into the hands of readers is truly a team effort. And I've had the privilege of playing with all-stars who also believe in the priceless value of character and integrity. I'm indebted to many people for believing in and sharpening *The Competitive Edge* so others can win more in life.

First, thank you Mavis Sanders. I didn't realize how our conversation in Boston would eventually affect my life in such a meaningful way. Thank you for being the perfect messenger.

Next, Jan Long Harris. I'm grateful for you—a keen, savvy visionary who lives by faith. I'm sure you already know that your leadership is highly respected and regarded by the rest of your team. Thank you for making me a part of the Tyndale family and encouraging this project from the beginning.

John Eames, my literary agent, my navigator, my handler. John, I appreciate your guidance and your seasoned ability to hit every pitch thrown at you. Thank you for including me on your roster and for working with a rookie like me.

Thank you also to Doug Knox and Jan Harris's powerhouse lineup of the Knox Group at Tyndale House: the camaraderie, knowledge, and talent of my editor Lisa Jackson; the efficiency, warmth, and humor of Sharon Leavitt; the attentive, meticulous, and devoted style of Sarah Atkinson; and the transparency, energy, and faithfulness of Yolanda Sidney.

My friend and mentor Sheila Heen, whose enthusiasm and encouragement is motivating. Sheila, I value your insight, wisdom, and can-do attitude. Thank you for challenging my thinking and letting me learn from you.

Another key player—Jay Lemke—a natural writer and new friend. Jay, thank you for your time, and for reading every word. Your generosity and willingness to give of yourself will be hard to repay. Thank you very much.

Curtis Cook and David Nazemi. Thank you for pinch-hitting in so many different ways in my life. Whether it was reading drafts, encouraging me, bringing humor to the situation, or brainstorming, you always come through with clutch hits and help me score. Thank you for your friendship and your character. You both are role models for me.

Special appreciation goes to many individuals who have been willing to share their lives through interviews so the rest of us can learn more about finding the competitive edge. Thank you Ed Carnett, Ernie Haase, Michael Moncrief, Rico Petrocelli, Dusty Rogers, Jim Spence, Jim Vitti, and Danny Wuerffel. I'm especially indebted to Curt Schilling and his publicist Katie Leighton, as well as Danny Wuerffel, his personal assistant Beverly Tillery, and the staff at Desire Street Ministries—all of whom have agreed that character and integrity should be a priority in life. Thank you for letting your character and integrity serve as examples to others.

On the home team, I'm thankful to my parents, Lowell and Gretchen Brown, for their support and encouragement in my personal and professional endeavors. They also helped me first grasp the understanding of what character and integrity are about. And finally, I'm thankful to my beautiful wife and best friend, Carolynne, who invested an hour for every hour that I did in this book. Carolynne, I love you for your patience, selflessness, encouragement, and loyalty. It took teamwork to get this book written, and you are no doubt my most valuable player.

FOREWORD

When I first met Jeff Brown, something just clicked. As I have gotten to know him, I found that he knows what he's talking about when it comes to character and integrity. This book is full of wisdom and insight into what it takes to win — but I'm not talking about winning at all costs.

Since the day I was born, my mother and father taught me what is most important in life. Winning is good, but the way you play the game is even more important. Some of my Gator fans may not believe this, but in the end, it's going to matter very little who won or by how much. It *is* going to make an eternal difference how the race was run. As a Christian, I believe that thinking and acting with integrity is absolutely critical in my relationship with God and with other people. I think a lot about the fact that most everything I do and say either brings glory to God or reflects poorly on me and Him.

A person's character really comes out during both the highs and the lows of life. Those of us who survived Hurricane Katrina and its devastating effects might say that the low points and hard times are the biggest challenge to moral and ethical behavior. During the days and weeks after the storm, I felt exhausted and discouraged and literally cried out to God to sustain me. But I have never felt closer to Him. At times like that, I really think that He is doing all the work because I don't have anything in myself left to give.

On the other hand, when things seem to be going really well and

I can see we're making good progress, I find I have to work harder to keep focused. It's easy to want to relax, let down my guard, and just kind of take it all in. (I'm not talking about physical rest here, although with a three-year-old and an eight-month-old baby in our house that sounds like a great idea!) The long process of recovering from Hurricane Katrina taught me that although reaching a peak is exciting, the valleys always come too. So I have to learn to pace my efforts and develop a sustainable balance that can carry me through the long run.

This book has so much good information in it, that if you only take away a little portion of it, you will still have gained a lot. I commend it to you with my encouragement to think about the eternal perspective and make your life here on earth count for the important things.

Danny Wuerffel

Former NFL quarterback

Destin, Florida

May, 2007

PREGAME WARM-UP

When was the last time you found yourself in a competitive situation? Not so long ago, serious competition was associated only with professional athletes on television or major corporate players assembled in a conference room with a spectacular view of a city. Well, the view has changed. Today, competition is commonplace; every day we find ourselves vying for some sort of prize. Maybe the prize is quality time with family or favorite friends. Maybe it's respect from coworkers and neighbors. Or perhaps it's simply making it through a barely red traffic light or choosing the shortest checkout line at the store. Whether we like it or not, we live in a world of competition and the game can be fierce.

Maybe you are an athlete or business leader who has had to ratchet up your skills in order to keep up with the demands of performance and productivity. Or perhaps you're a parent, teacher, or pastor who feels pressured to take your personal game to the next level. The compelling urge to compete is real and can't be ignored. As a faculty member at Harvard Medical School and McLean Hospital for nearly a decade, I've had the fortunate opportunity to consult with a variety of athletes, businesspeople, entrepreneurs, students, professors, and colleagues who feel the intense pressure of performance and competition in their lives daily. Every day you get yourself out of bed, out the door, and off to work, the temptation to sacrifice your integrity is staring you down. Our competitive culture has effectively duped many people into believing that regardless of how we play the game of life, any strategy is acceptable as long as we win. Whether in the boardroom or athletic arena, at home or school, in the pulpit or the carpool, you're in the game too.

Everyone is playing the game. Everyone wants to win—no matter the cost. And it's clear that countless people *still* seem to think that nice guys are doomed to finish last. In many competitive situations, character and personal integrity are simply regarded as old-fashioned strategies for climbing one's way to the top. They are frequently undervalued as being too conservative, clear signs of weakness, or simply a waste of time.

If competition were a virus, we would have an epidemic on our hands. Have you noticed any symptoms of the outbreak around you? The evidence is everywhere: colleagues frantically grabbing for the next rung on the corporate ladder, rookies claiming overstated accomplishments on their résumés, athletes using drugs to improve performance, white-collar corruption around every corner, businesspeople cultivating shallow relationships just to get an advantage.

For Christians, however, life isn't supposed to feel like a contest—even though on many days it does. God has already given us the ultimate rule book, one that shows us how to win every time we play. Christians are not only to enjoy life, but enjoy it abundantly. And God doesn't need for us to cheat so that His will can be accomplished in our lives. When it comes to competition, His rules place character and integrity above everything else. By keeping character and integrity intact, you'll never compete *against* God for His will in your life.

It's easy to become distracted by trophies, money, promotions, and attention. So if we want to guard against grabbing the low-hanging fruit, we must realize that we're in this game for the long haul. But this doesn't mean you will never be a winner. It simply means that you'll win the *right* way: according to God's plan for your life. Proverbs tells us that a person who has integrity also possesses wisdom, understanding, mercy, and favor from God. When we follow His rules, using character and integrity to win, victories are translated into spiritual strength.

Each spring I don the hat of sport psychologist for the Boston Marathon medical team. At the finish line in Boston's Copley Square, I consult with runners who have trained for months in preparation for the holy grail of marathons. They feel the intense, do-whatever-it-takes pressure of competition. Whether daily in my private practice or once a year at the finish line of a major sporting event, clients often tell me they struggle to make the right decisions when faced with situations where their values can be compromised. Some are satisfied with a decision to stick with their values, while others regret later that they gave in so quickly. Athletes and businesspeople who have confidence in their character and values still find themselves going head-to-head with cutthroat competitors too. Regardless of whose integrity and character are compromised, the sweet taste of victory can still have a bitter aftertaste of guilt, shame, regret, or compromise.

Max was a runner I met at the Boston Marathon. By the time we were introduced, he was already having both legs iced and he was in tears. His physical pain, however, didn't compare to his emotional pain. Max described his emotional aftertaste to me. You see, Max had forfeited hundreds of hours with his wife and kids so he could train for the marathon. He had numerous discussions with his wife that flared into arguments about his priorities with her and with their children. While that conflict was occurring, Max had also been advised by his physician to avoid running lengthy races because his previous knee injuries would almost certainly be aggravated in both legs. Max didn't want to hear his doctor's advice, nor did he consider the pleas from his wife. He wanted to run the marathon for himself. He wanted the bragging rights, he wanted the admiration, he wanted his friends and colleagues to talk about him, he wanted his kids to be proud of him and tell their friends at school.

With five miles left to go in the marathon, Max's legs began making a crackling noise and literally stopped working. He couldn't run; he couldn't even crawl. Race volunteers brought him to the medical tent, where he had no other option but to consider how his decision to nurture his ego would now affect his wife, his children, and his character. He regretted his shallow priorities and was ashamed that he placed his superficial ego needs over his family. Max's bitter aftertaste was only washed away later by his family's forgiveness. It was a tough lesson to learn, but Max finally realized that the lure of accolades was not worth compromising his integrity and character. Given the state of our competitive culture and the indisputable truth that most people want to win at all costs, you must bulletproof yourself against the temptation to play by the wrong set of rules. As a person of faith, you have an extra resource — a competitive edge — in this fight to do right over wrong.

After conducting several thousand hours of therapy with clients, I've come to learn at least seven basic, yet crucial, principles that can guide every serious competitor to victory every time he or she competes. Those seven principles make up the competitive edge that strengthens your character and integrity in a world where traditional values, sportsmanship, and a good work ethic are undervalued and frequently mocked. When it comes to competing, your character and integrity will be under daily attack. You will either sacrifice your integrity at the great cost of losing face with yourself and others, or you'll increase your confidence and faith by being a legitimate winner every time your character is challenged in competition. When you pull all of the principles together, you've found your competitive edge. *The Competitive Edge* will give you an advantage over the competition by giving you vital principles that you can use to guide your character toward victory. If you are a champion, you can win every time you compete.

Make no mistake: Success has many different faces. So don't think your character and integrity are of any less value because the final outcome isn't as significant as you want it to be. Whether it's winning the Stanley Cup or selling the most cupcakes at a school fund-raiser, your character and integrity are of equal importance.

Maybe you think you already have your integrity game face on and that you are not like other competitors who are apt to throw integrity under the bus just to get ahead. Do you consider yourself a winner? If so, do you dream of endorsing an athletic company's new line of clothing? Or desire to be a spokesperson for a charity that you believe in with all of your heart? Maybe you think you'd look chic on a trendy magazine or on the evening news. If you've ever felt a buzz from the lure of celebrity status, you're in good company. Many people like the idea of fame. You should also know that you are just as vulnerable to compromising your character and integrity as anyone else.

You know the signs of a big winner: glossy photos, tell-all book deals, dream salaries, newspaper headlines, gated-community living, speaking tours, and a table of your choice in any restaurant you choose. These are the images of fame and success for those who are declared winners by societal standards. Don't ignore what is going on around you. Don't think for a minute that your character and integrity aren't at risk. We live in the reality of stiff competition, and everyone wishes they could be the champ. Even if you're already competing on the side of character and integrity, you can sharpen your competitive edge so you won't be sucked under by the current of extreme competition.

Many people want to be a champion so badly that they can think about nothing else. Just the sound of it — *top dog, numero uno, the big cheese* — can make anyone want to be an admired VIP. Your character and integrity should rise above the fading limelight. It should be more highly valued than a tarnishing bronze trophy or tattered blue ribbon because trophies and ribbons don't influence children. They don't encourage friends. They don't honor spouses. They don't stand up for what is right. They don't last in meaningful ways like character and integrity do. Why spend time investing in temporary fame when you can have lasting victory from day to day?

If you develop your competitive edge, winning can happen every time you compete. Let the guiding principles of the *competitive edge* lead you to victory, regardless of the outcome. Whether you compete against others in sport or business, or compete against yourself to reach personal goals, the means by which you win will reflect your true character — the core of who you are. Even when you stand alone, you will still be a champion.

Know the Rules of the Game

I try not to break the rules, but merely to test their elasticity.
Bill Veeck
MLB owner, 1991 National Baseball Hall of Fame inductee

One afternoon in my office, I sat in an after-school session with Sean, a fifth-grader who was having trouble getting along with his friends, parents, and teachers. He had a reputation for being a stubborn bully and clearly didn't think highly of himself. His self-esteem was low, and he knew that people didn't really like him. I wanted to connect with him so we could eventually have some conversations about tough topics. Sean said he was glad to be in my office and took himself on a self-guided tour before accepting my offer to play a game of Electronic Battleship.

Sean said he was familiar with the game but that no one had ever been willing to play with him before. After firing missiles back and forth for a few minutes, I sank one of Sean's vessels by chance. He immediately stood up, tossed the game to the floor, and stormed out of my office. I found Sean sitting by himself in the waiting room with his arms crossed, staring at the floor. I sat across from him, and together we waited in silence. After a few minutes, Sean glared at me and blurted out: "You didn't tell me the rules. Now you sunk my boat and made me lose the game." I thanked Sean for expressing his thoughts and feelings about losing and invited him to return to my office, where we would review the rules together. He was relieved to know that losing one boat didn't mean losing the game.

Sean isn't the only one feeling the need to win these days. Just as Sean needed to know the rules of the game he was playing, it's important for us to know the rules of our game as well. Without knowing the boundaries and rules of a competition, it's easy to become emotionally off balance and compromise integrity while trying to salvage a victory. When we know we are under-informed, feelings of inadequacy come to the surface quickly. That alone can be embarrassing, deflating, and unfair. We want to perform well, so we may be tempted to take shortcuts in order to compensate for what we don't know.

> *Rules were made to be broken.*
>
> Anonymous

Parents of a teenager I see in therapy wanted their son to be well-prepared for his college entrance exams, so they hired a tutor to help him. Their son met with the tutor several times before his parents discovered that the tutor was also teaching him how to cheat by using a cell phone, iPod, and other technical devices. Up to this point, the parents had not realized just how intensely competitive these exams could be, and to what lengths people would go in order to succeed. Even the tutor compromised integrity to improve his own reputation as a teacher. They never intended for their son to cheat in order to elevate his test scores; they simply didn't understand the rules some people play by in the college entrance exam game.

If you are going to be good at a game, you must have a clear understanding of the rules. Sometimes beginner's luck can make others think you have natural talent, but they won't be fooled for long. Whether your personal playing field is athletics or business, academics or politics, church or parenting, you'll surely remain an amateur if you have only a vague sense of how your game is played. In order to become a pro, you must understand all of the rules, as well as how and why the game is played. In fact, not knowing the complete parameters of a sport or business can put you in a bind, particularly when your character and integrity are on the line.

Know the Details of the Rules

UCLA coaching legend John Wooden once said, "When you see a successful individual, a 'winner,' a champion, you can be sure that you are looking at an individual who pays great attention to the perfection of minor details."

Coach Wooden's comment reminds me of a woman named Rebecca whom I consulted in my office. She had recently gotten married and joined a prestigious law firm. One afternoon, Rebecca came to her session and asked me to give her feedback about a decision she had made. Earlier in the week, she had received her first six-month employee evaluation. She met with a partner in the firm, who delivered a

> *When you see a successful individual, a champion, you can be very sure that you are looking at an individual who pays great attention to the perfection of minor details.*
>
> John Wooden
> UCLA coaching legend

stellar performance review, emphasizing her enthusiasm and praising her intelligence and dependability. The partner went so far as to suggest that with some minor improvements, Rebecca could easily be on track to make partner after a few years.

Rebecca asked how she could improve her job performance, and the partner told her that even though she was already billing many hours, she still wasn't generating enough income for the firm. Rebecca quickly read between the lines. It was clear that if she wanted to be in line for a promotion, she needed to bill more hours.

Rebecca had planned to balance work and professional growth with her family life. But the rules she thought she was playing by had changed. She was already working nearly eighty hours a week, and there simply wasn't enough of her to go around. She would now have to decide what values were more important to her — work or family.

Rebecca's heart sank and she left the partner's office disappointed, both in the firm and in herself. She was disappointed in the firm because, although it had a highly regarded reputation in the business world, its main motivation was money. Second, she was disappointed she hadn't learned all of the firm's rules before she accepted the job. To her credit, she *had* asked a variety of good questions during her pre-job interviews, but the business practices she discovered were not divulged until now.

Rebecca decided the rules the firm followed and the rules she used to define her character were appreciably different. She could not allow herself to build a career by sacrificing family values in the name of greed.

Rebecca didn't really need my approval for her decision that day. She made a sound decision to avoid putting a price tag on her character. After that, she stayed with the firm, only one more month, billing hours that honestly reflected the time that she worked. She later transitioned to a different firm, where the rules were more explicit and individual values took priority over cash flow.

I'm guessing that Coach Wooden would say that Rebecca was a champion, even if she was perhaps a slow learner. Because she didn't initially have all of the rules of the game, she had to learn them the hard way.

Know the Value of Your Integrity

If you've picked up this book because you want to have another set of strategies for beating the competition and coming out on top financially, you might as well put it back down or give it to a friend. On second thought, perhaps you should keep reading. You may discover more internal wealth than you ever knew you could possess. This book was written to help you protect your integrity and character, neither of which should bear a price tag—but they frequently do.

As you read on, you must ask yourself these questions: Is my character important to me? Is integrity a word I want others to use when they describe me? Do I want others to know I stand on personal principle? When it's all said and done, can I be satisfied that I stood for what I believed?

It can be tough to resist the temptation to compromise character, because winning feels good and is highly admired culturally. Clients often share with me stories of envy, frustration, and anger over the heavy-handed competitors they face in their daily lives. Sometimes they even fantasize about infecting their foe's computer with a virus, or circulating a memo that reflects errors in their colleague's work and calls into question that person's judgment. These fantastic, often unreasonable schemes usually soften after a good discussion about what matters most to my clients. In some cases, the old appeal, "Do you really want to stoop to their level?" can still assuage the urge to "get even."

But let's be honest. Sometimes it feels much better to justify revenge and settle the score in a selfish way than it does to delay the gratification of watching your competition bite the dust. When you have to deal with an inflammatory teammate, colleague, or boss, the problem is not your anger about the situation, but it's what you *do* with that anger that affects your character.

I continue to be amazed that many Christians still believe anger is a sin. Anger is simply one of many God-given emotions that humans have. Even Jesus became angry when He saw the money changers in the Temple. But when we use anger as justification for our own bad behavior, we damage our integrity.

When someone provokes you to anger—and they will—when you know all you can about your personal playing field, you have a better chance of staying on your toes in a defensive stance, ready to respond. Once you know the rules, you'll be more equipped to recognize assaults on your character and decision making.

Can you can recall a time when your character was challenged by an opponent and you were tempted to sacrifice your integrity for a win? If so, you deserve to be congratulated. Why, you ask? Because your opponent saw you as a challenge. He or she was convinced that you were worth beating and that a victory over you was important. If your character isn't under attack, then you probably aren't really participating in the game anyway.

Guard Your Integrity with Knowledge

Regardless of their faith orientation, most competitors would agree with Proverbs 24:5: "A wise man has great power, and a man of knowledge increases strength." Does the Schoolhouse Rock mantra "knowledge is power" resonate with you? Even unethical competitors live by this Sir Francis Bacon quote. Every competitor seeks knowledge, information, and strategy in an effort to gain the upper hand. They can be your competitors, your teammates, your supervisors, your employees. Don't be paranoid; not everyone we play against or do business with is a bad guy. But let's be honest — character and integrity aren't at the top of everybody's priority list.

Regardless of whether or not character and integrity are priorities for them, many competitors think the more they know, the more they will win. They tell themselves they will get a bigger salary with more power and prestige. They want to supervise more people and long for greater respect. They want their coach to call on them first. They want to own the limelight.

By increasing your knowledge of your sport, your business, your field, or your specialty, you can insulate your character against unethical competitors and preserve your value-based integrity at the same time. Think of knowledge in the same way you think of rules in a game. The more you know about a game, the more expert you will become. The more expert you become, the more you will play at advanced levels. Ecclesiastes 7:12 guarantees, "the advantage of knowledge is that wisdom preserves the lives of its possessors" (NASB). When your character remains intact, you will win big every time.

Be Prepared for the Rules to Change

For well over a century, the Harvard and Yale football teams have faced off each fall in what is known as "The Game." As with most rivalries, these Ivy League schools are rich with tradition and have obvious enthusiasm for this gridiron clash. Similarly, just down the Charles River from the Harvard campus is the Massachusetts Institute of Technology (MIT), where another tradition of sorts is alive and well.

For years, MIT students have stolen the focus of The Game by designing a prank that relies on perfect timing and the element of surprise—not to mention intelligence and creativity. T. F. Peterson confirms in his book *Nightwork* that Harvard and Yale players should be on guard, because the playing field can change at a moment's notice when MIT students are on the prowl. Pranks have included a rocket soaring over the football goalpost with an MIT banner in tow, an inflatable MIT-tattooed weather balloon that eventually exploded on the playing field, and crowd participation activities that deliver a punch line aimed at unsuspecting Harvardians—led of course, by MIT students disguised as Crimson loyalists.

The lesson here is to expect rules to change, particularly when a rival or competitor has an agenda other than your own. So maybe you don't play for Harvard, Yale, or MIT, but you do expect people to keep their word when they agree to do something. When they don't follow through, their integrity and character come into question, and it's not so funny. These collegiate antics are done in the name of cleverness and old-fashioned entertainment, but when the rules change in the workplace, the motive is often money, prestige, or influence. The stakes can be much higher, and rules can be adjusted to fit an unethical competitor's agenda without notice to you.

Search Out Good Role Models

How many classes have you ever taken that focused on integrity, character, or principle? I'd guess not too many. Maybe you had an ethics class at some point while pursuing your education. If you sat in such a class for very long, you probably participated in a debate over whether ethics can be taught to someone. That discussion usually ended with an agreement that ethical principles can be learned as a set of rules, but they won't always reflect the values a person actually has. I would agree with that notion.

While many theories for learning exist, social learning theory seems to be one useful perspective for understanding learning in our culture. Eminent psychologist and Stanford professor Albert Bandura identified that people learn behaviors or modify current behaviors by observing someone else doing it first. For example, a coach might yell at a referee following an apparent bad call at a game. By watching the coach yell at the ref, players learn to express their anger using poor sportsmanship, a negative behavior. The next time a bad call occurs, the players are now apt to yell at the official.

In another example, a child may observe one parent who lies to the other parent about something insignificant. Now the child has learned that telling an untruth is acceptable. On more grown-up terms, a boss who encourages an employee to embellish services or make empty promises to gain business is teaching his novice supervisee fraudulent business tactics. Remember the line from the children's song that says, "Oh, be careful, little eyes, what you see?" I'm sure Bandura didn't write the lyrics, but he would likely agree that we learn rules about how to behave by watching and listening to others.

You may not even realize it when you are being exposed to images or behaviors that later influence your character. Modeling can occur before you know it's happening to you. The media has created a reality entertainment niche by setting high stakes for people who are willing to compete. *Survivor, The Apprentice,* and *The Amazing Race* are all part of our cultural vocabularies now. We even know many of the players by name. Viewers watch intensely competitive episodes built on a simple formula that includes ruthless strategy and a big payoff. How often have you seen a contestant lie about a relative dying, a friend having a terminal illness, financial ruin, or some other fabricated tragedy offered with an honest face? Contestants often form alliances with other contestants, only to find out later that their loyalty to each other was a ruse used in the name of strategy. Unfortunately, some shows use this self-defamation of character to generate a loyal fan base and keep viewers coming back for more.

Reality television might have had some devoted viewers in biblical times. Commercials would have sounded something like, "You won't believe the lengths that Jacob will go to scam his blind father, Isaac, out of the family blessing. Watch next week to see how Jacob's actions change their family forever."

In Luke 10, the parable of the Good Samaritan serves as a clear example of how one man wasn't influenced by the popular culture of his day. Instead, he chose to disregard cultural norms and help a Jewish man who had been left for dead along a road, even after a priest and a Levite had passed the injured man by. The Samaritan and Jew were radically different from one other — racially, socially, and financially. They had nothing in common except a relationship in which each overlooked what their culture had defined for them. Scripture is replete with individuals who can still serve as role models for us today: Noah demonstrated faith, Job showed patience when life got tough, Ruth was kind, and Abraham was generous. If your role models don't possess integrity, it's time to find new ones.

Keep Your Head in the Game

The Yucatán Peninsula is home to Chichén Itzá, a historically powerful Mayan civilization whose massive stone structures remain relatively intact. For all practical purposes, Chichén Itzá looks much like it did hundreds of years ago, with the exception of crumbling rocks and deeper crevices chiseled away by centuries of wind and rain. When visiting there a few years ago, I was awed by an enormous centerpiece pyramid called El Castillo that towers above Chichén Itzá. Visitors can still climb the narrow steps to the top of the pyramid if they think they are up to it. If you need to balance yourself for the dizzying descent, a rope is there to hold on to.

While El Castillo is an architectural wonder in its own right, I have to admit my strongest memory of the sultry 103-degree tour of Chichén Itzá was the expansive ball court located just northwest of the massive pyramid. It was a vast sporting arena that would have served as a perfect backdrop for an *Indiana Jones and the Temple of Whatever* movie. There in the echoing ball court, our veteran tour guide and lifelong Chichén Itzá native, Alfredo, described the gaming history of the Mayan people and their great love of competition. Their loyalty to sports was more than impressive.

Among the sports they played, the Maya played a game called pok-ta-pok. It seems there are a few theories about how pok-ta-pok was played. Some historians believe it was a cross between soccer and basketball, with a bit of head-to-head football thrown in. Etched inside the walls of the pok-ta-pok courts are stone carvings of athletes in various poses. Alfredo pointed out a particular carving of one headless athlete who had seven snakes coming out of his neck, then asked our unsuspecting group of tourists to guess the symbolism of that figure. After a few reasonable guesses by his sweaty onlookers, Alfredo explained we were looking at the captain of the winning — not the losing — team. He had been decapitated as a sign of honor and respect for being the champion. The seven snake heads growing out of the captain's neck supposedly pleased the Mayan gods.

I immediately knew that sport psychology would have had no real meaningful place in Mayan culture. Can you imagine being a sport psychologist who was consulting with a pok-ta-pok captain and establishing goals for working together? "So you want to get your head lobbed off? . . . I see." If you ask me, second place sounds pretty inviting. Not all rules make sense.

As we continued with the tour of the ruins, I mulled over this notion of losing one's head for winning. Surely, I thought, the captain didn't understand the rules. Maybe the captain was somehow a prisoner set up to die in the name of entertainment. On a deeper level, I tried empathizing with the values of the Mayan people and the strong desire they had to please their gods. For them, winning was an incredible sacrifice.

Isn't it interesting to think about what motivates us to compete in our world today? We might not have our heads chopped off, but we may be more like the Mayan culture than we think. In athletics, in the business world, or in other cultural arenas, we are frequently offered opportunities to lay priceless possessions — such as personal principles and values — on the line. How many times have you or a colleague or a teammate had character and integrity lobbed off in the name of winning? Just as we need to know the rules of the game, we also need to be very clear about what the payoff will be. Knowing our rules will help us strategize our next move. Knowing where that move will take us will help us to decide whether we want to play the game in the first place. Do we really want to place our character on the chopping block?

Be Willing to Change Your Perspective

It was a Saturday evening in late winter. My wife was out of town visiting relatives, so I had the opportunity to be a bachelor again. For a few years, I had wanted to make a trek to Lowell, Massachusetts, to watch its minor-league hockey team in person. Regardless of the sport, minor league games tend to be family-oriented, allow for crowd participation, and offer the chance for kids to meet a favorite player. The atmosphere is fun-filled — particularly with hockey. It didn't take much thought before I jumped into my Jeep and blazed a trail to the arena, where I hoped to get a decent seat, enjoy the energy of the local crowd, and indulge in unhealthy food.

My plan turned out to be a pretty good one. Logistically, I couldn't have scored any better. I arrived as the national anthem was cranking up. After clicking around on her computer keyboard — just after "the rockets' red glare" — the box office clerk said she had a single seat in the best section of the arena. I eagerly paid her and took the ticket for Section A, Row 1, Seat 1. Perfect. My seat was against the glass, with a fan-pleasing view of the game. This tall barrier of unbreakable glass surrounded the rink to contain the game and to prevent any airborne pucks—or players for that matter—from colliding into the fans. I looked to my right. The penalty box! Not only could I see the action, but I had also purchased the chance of becoming seatmates with some of the most aggressive players on the ice.

As great as my seat was, it wasn't all perfect. I didn't realize that while sitting in Section A, Row 1, Seat 1, I ran the risk of having my evening meal destroyed by an audience participation game called Chuck-A-Puck (not to be confused with the Mayan favorite, pok-ta-pok). The announcer yelled over the public address system, "Chuck your pucks!" and a downpour of foam rubber hockey pucks started falling on the ice.

The pucks flew from the luxury boxes, the general admission section, and the food court area. I figured everyone must be aiming at some sort of target and that a lucrative prize was probably guaranteed for the puck chucker who had the best strategy and most amount of luck. The bad news for me was that two women behind me seemed to be shooting better than the hockey team that night as they each chucked their puck into my chicken strip basket with pinpoint accuracy. In fact, the second woman's intensity for winning the big prize was so strong that she came down to Row 1, Seat 1 to retrieve her puck in order to throw it again. I warned her that throwing the now barbeque-sauce-soaked puck could be a pretty messy ordeal, especially once it hit the ice. She reluctantly agreed, apologized for adding another course to my meal, and went back to her seat.

So is there any good news about Section A, Row 1, Seat 1? It's not actually about the seat, but the perspective the seat gave me. A great seat didn't keep me from possible harm.

Just like character, rules keep us safe even when we don't know it. About eight minutes into the first period, I noticed a boy in the next section over get up from his fifth-row seat and run proudly down to the glass to pose for a photo. He was sporting a hockey jersey and logo hat. It was clear by the expression on his face and his price-tag adorned shirt that he was a hockey scene "newbie" who was thrilled to be at the game.

He turned around with his back to the protective glass, smiling at his mother's camera lens. At the same moment the camera flash went off, two of the hockey players who were wedged together trying to get at the puck slammed against the glass behind the boy. The crowd yelled, saliva flew from one player's mouth, his sweaty arms and an unshaven face flattened against the glass – just behind the smiling kid. Don't worry, the glass didn't break. In fact, within seconds the situation was over. The safety glass worked just like it was supposed to, and the child never knew he was literally inches from danger. Just like the glass safeguarded the young fan, our personal rules keep our character and integrity from being bruised and broken.

Like that safety glass, our rules may not be obvious or stand out, but when we're under attack, they offer a shield of protection, keeping us from harm and danger. Others may not notice these rules until they slam into them. The kid at the hockey game was protected by the safety glass and never knew how close he was to being hurt. For many of my clients, integrity works just like the safety glass at the hockey rink. If it's in place, they are fully protected and may never even know it.

Know the Rules of the Game

Just like Sean who learned to play Electronic Battleship with me, we've come to see the importance of rules and how they affect the way we play the game. After Sean understood the rules and what to expect, his relationship with me improved. Even more important, his relationships with friends and family deepened. They didn't deepen because Sean became a better Battleship player, but because he learned that he possessed character.

In today's world, the phrase "rules were made to be broken" has probably never been truer. However, when we learn the rules of our game, establish our own rules, and learn to respond when others break the rules, our character and integrity are strengthened and win out.

Eleanor Roosevelt once said, "Somehow, we learn who we really are and then live with that decision." By knowing the rules well, you'll be better prepared to respond to situations where your integrity could be compromised, attacked, or exploited. When you know the rules of the game you are playing as thoroughly as you know the rules of your personal values, you are on the right path to becoming a capable competitor.

POSTGAME REVIEW

- ✕ Learn the rules of your game as well as or better than your opponent knows them.
- ✕ Don't assume the rules are obvious; ask for details.
- ✕ Make sure character and integrity are actual priorities before you compete.
- ✕ Know how you will respond when rules change unexpectedly.
- ✕ Find good role models and watch them closely.
- ✕ Remember daily the true value of character and integrity.

Recognize the Right
Decision and Make It

*We need people who influence their peers and who
cannot be detoured from their convictions by peers
who do not have the courage to have any convictions.*

Joe Paterno
Penn State University football coach

Life is full of questions. Questions like "Should I take the new job
even though I'll have to move?" "Should I talk with the coach about
my scholarship for next year?" "Should I get married now and
bypass living overseas?" Keeping decision making simple is usually the best course of action. Tough decisions require thoughtful
solutions. Not every solution is perfect.

Perched on a shelf in my study is a replica of the original walnut
and glass sign that sat on President Harry Truman's desk in the Oval
Office. The sign reads "I'm from Missouri" on one side and "The
Buck Stops Here" on the other. It was made in 1945 in the United
States Federal Reformatory in El Reno, Oklahoma, at the request of
U.S. Marshal Fred Canfil, a friend of President Truman's. Truman
often referred to that sign in speeches, particularly when he made a
point about responsibility and accountability in decision making.

It's not uncommon for people to blame others for a bad decision, even when it's one that they made themselves. Players blame coaches, bosses blame employees, kids blame parents — and vice versa. Either laughingly or with shallow sincerity, some of my nonpsychotic clients have discounted their bad choices to compromise integrity by saying, "Satan tempted me." The longer I practice, the less I buy the idea that the devil forces people to behave badly. It's time we realize that each one of us has the power to make choices. We must use this power wisely, and then take responsibility for the choices that we make.

I once heard a story about a politician who was presented with an ethical dilemma. The politician had nearly finished his first term in office and was getting ready to run for reelection. His campaign manager came to him and told him a particular wealthy family had agreed to pay half of the construction costs for a new bridge in one of the state's counties. The contributing family had political influence and expected the bridge would be named in honor of the person of their choosing. While the family would pay for half of the bridge expense, the remaining half of the cost would have to be "found" in the existing state operating budget.

> *Two roads diverged in a wood, and I . . . took the one less traveled by, and that has made all the difference.*
> Robert Frost
> American poet

After analyzing the budget, the politician's staff informed him that the money for completing the bridge project would need to be taken from funds already allocated for education. The politician wouldn't hear of it. He decided to keep the money for education in place, even though doing so might jeopardize his bid for reelection. "I'd rather be right than elected," he told his staff members. As the story goes, the politician won the election.

Sometimes preserving character and integrity means forfeiting our professional goals and aspirations.

Is Your Character for Sale?

When making daily decisions, people often fail to realize the intrinsic value of character and integrity. You can't go to the store to buy new integrity, and you can't order new character on the Internet. What you possess now is what you will die with. Its value depends on how you invest it throughout your life, what you trade it for, and how often you give it away.

When Robert takes a ream of paper from his office to use in his printer at home, he is selling his integrity for the price of inexpensive copy paper. I'd like to know why he was willing to sell off his character so cheaply.

If you've ever hosted a rummage sale and tried to sell your leftover stuff, you'll remember the tedious task of marking sticky price tags for each item. It's not the writing that's the challenge — it's the process of deciding how much you want for each piece of junk. Take, for example, the used soccer ball gathering dust in the back of your closet. When you appraise it, you consider its condition and appearance. You might even touch up the scuff marks to give it more curb appeal. Adding some air wouldn't hurt, either. As you hold that ball, you begin to recall the great goals or blocks that you once made, leading up to a season-ending championship trophy. Amusingly, the value continues to increase as you think about how important that ball really is to you. Some shopper will be lucky to own such a valuable find. At this point, will anyone be able to afford it?

The truth is that most of us spend more time thinking about the value of worn sporting equipment, out-of-style clothing, Tupperware pieces, and cassette tapes than integrity and character. But isn't the value of your character worth considering more than the bent snow shovel you haven't used in five years? Isn't it worth exploring the meaning and value of character and its potential use to others? We need to consider these factors and make a decision about what price tag — if any — should be placed on character and integrity.

Just like Robert and the ream of copy paper, you can measure the financial value of your character by the monetary gain that results from each decision you make. When you realize each decision you make has a value, you learn to keep the worth of your character and integrity in perspective. In Robert's case, his integrity is valued at about ten bucks — the cost of a ream of paper. How often do we fail to put a value label on the things that are most important? Of course we can't walk around with a yard sale tag stuck to us, but we can label the value of our character with our words, actions, and attitudes. When we fail to let people know how much we value integrity, we may as well be sending the message: "Make me an offer."

Every day you are faced with choices — choices that may define your career and definitely will define your *character*. Be prepared: Making the choice to do what is right means that you will risk criticism — no matter if you are right or wrong. Making the right choice when faced with a tough decision — and then standing by it — can either make or break your image. It's up to you to decide if it's worth it.

In the name of equal rights, Rosa Parks made a decision and

refused to give up her seat on a bus in Montgomery, Alabama. Her choice was costly — her freedom when she was arrested — but it was a price she was willing to pay because she knew the true worth of her values. And because of that decision, people of all races still benefit today. That's quite valuable, wouldn't you say?

A Silent Fumble with Major Penalties

Andrew was a senior offensive guard who played football at a midwestern university. For him, football was not just a game. Football represented family and tradition. His brother had played on the team five years before, and his father had played when he attended the same school thirty years earlier. Andrew had had a decent college career so far, one he could be proud of — one that would add to the family history books.

However, an incident occurred during his senior year that he couldn't shake. The weekend before the home opener, some of the upperclassmen started a new initiation tradition for the freshmen players. One of the cocaptains decided to have all twelve freshmen drink mixed alcohol concoctions, randomly placed in front of the players by the upperclassmen. The hazing would stop when the first freshman threw up. Though all of the players were adults, Andrew knew they were underage for drinking. Even though Andrew wasn't a drinker himself, he knew that the random drinks game posed some possible physical risks too. He felt compelled to derail the prank but didn't. Andrew didn't want to risk being embarrassed and losing respect as a senior player.

The initiation began as planned and continued until the first freshman vomited. There were pats on the back, uproarious cheering, and "attaboys," before the team called it a night. Nobody realized, however, that one freshman had drunk way too much. He staggered to his dorm room, passed out on his bed, and was found gravely ill by his roommate the next morning. The player was hospitalized for alcohol poisoning. News of the freshman's condition circulated quickly through the team in the locker room. Andrew was filled with regret for not speaking out against what he knew was wrong. The price tag he placed on embarrassment could have been the same price he placed on someone's life. His appraisal was clearly wrong.

Some decisions require you to take risks and then live with your choice. In order to follow through with your decision, you may have to be comfortable with the uncomfortable feelings that risks create.

Multiple pressures will come into play when it comes to decision making, particularly if the decision could affect finances, social status, or other people. The trouble for most of us is that we don't want to make a wrong decision about doing the right thing. Losing sleep, visualizing various scenarios in your mind, asking friends for their opinions, developing a painful headache, and nursing mild nausea are all signs of decision-making stress.

Yes, decision making carries risk, risk that may involve money, popularity, humiliation, isolation, status, or rejection. Some of these are the very factors that keep us from making the right decision even when we know better. Peter knew how much Jesus loved him and had done for him, but he also knew that acknowledging their relationship would be dangerous and humiliating—possibly even leading to his own death. Peter chose the safer route and denied Jesus three separate times.

We've known for years that hindsight is 20/20. If Peter was honest, he would probably admit that he knew denying Jesus was wrong. He simply lacked the courage to make the right decision. But that right decision could have saved Peter a lifetime of regret. In the long run, which decision do you suppose had the greater value? When you do make an integrity-based decision, don't keep it to yourself. An old German proverb says, "Better silent than stupid." Perhaps a less risky phrase is the Mark Twain credo: "It is better to keep your mouth closed and let people think you are a fool than to open it and remove all doubt." When it comes to matters of integrity, I would not live by these standards. Just like Andrew and his football team's hazing, negative consequences occur when we don't give integrity a voice. How many times have you heard someone say that they regret not having spoken up about something that was important? For whatever reason, they opted not to let their values be known.

From the Psychology Hall of Fame

So, why are ethical choices so hard to make? It may have more to do with the type of person making the decision than the decisions themselves. When it comes to competition, it can be helpful to understand some basic personality theories. What makes people tick? What does your opponent really want in life? What exactly is he or she trying to accomplish?

Two prominent psychologists have contributed significant information to the current understanding of personality, giving us some insight into how people make decisions.

Alfred Adler: Striving for superiority

Alfred Adler was a well-known twentieth-century European psychologist who carved out his own personality theory called individual psychology. Individual psychology came during an era when

Sigmund Freud's psychoanalytic theory was thriving. Adler agreed with Freud about the importance of early childhood experiences in some instances. However, Adler focused more on an individual's attempt to shape his or her future, rather than trying to unravel the negative experiences of the past. For this reason alone, Adler's theory stands as a good explanation of how making a difficult decision and sticking with it, even when it's not a popular one, can shape our lives and character.

"Striving for superiority," as Adler called it, is a person's way of trying to be good, have meaning, or be perfect. Striving, however, can be manifested in various strategies that may or may not reflect character. This notion of being good and having meaning in life sounds so easy, but it's not simple at all. You see, *striving* is a verb, an action word, which implies that it's ongoing. Adler didn't suggest people strive only on Mondays, Wednesdays, and Fridays, taking the other days off. Striving goes on daily in our decisions, behaviors, and relationships — seven days a week.

David, a college student in Phoenix, was one of a dozen employees who worked weekends at an enormous movie complex. David's responsibilities included selling tickets, running one of the four concession stands, and picking up empty soda cups and popcorn tubs at the end of each night. He enjoyed being a theater employee. He worked with a wonderful group of people. Everyone there helped each other so they all could finish work on time. When David finished his own tasks, he often vacuumed the hallways for his coworker Tim. Tim was thin and always seemed to be in a rush. As they got to know each other, David learned that Tim was working three jobs in order to pay rent and buy groceries for his wife and two kids.

During a Saturday morning staff meeting at the theater, David's manager brought up the issue of free ticket vouchers. According to the theater policy, each worker received two movie passes a month for friends and family. Since many of the employees had access to tickets, the policy operated on an honor system. However, the shift manager explained that more than a hundred passes had been taken by employees during the last week. Most of the employees were surprised; who would have taken so many tickets? No one's job was in jeopardy, the manager explained, but the theater owner was considering discontinuing the benefit if the rules for the passes continued to be broken.

After the meeting, David offered Tim a ride to his next job. In the car, Tim confided that he had been taking the movie passes from the ticket office and selling them to friends at a discount to make extra money. He still had ten passes. "David," Tim said, "could you help me? Could you slip into the ticket office and put these tickets back? I can't afford to lose this job.

> *To believe in something and not to live it is dishonest.*
> Ghandi
> Author, attorney, and
> social activist

No one would hold it against you, if you were caught bending the rules. Everyone likes you because you're so helpful."

In Tim's opinion, David's character had the value of ten movie passes and the opportunity to help a friend. David believed his character was worth much more, but he knew Tim would never realize that if he didn't speak up now. David decided to help Tim, but suggested a way to do it that wouldn't sacrifice his own values in the process.

"You need to go to the shift manager and explain your financial situation," David said to Tim. "I'll go with you." He believed the shift manager's word that no one would lose his job. Not only did David give moral support to Tim, he offered to work an extra shift a week to help pay for the vouchers Tim had taken. This offer increased the value of David's character not only in Tim's eyes, but also in the shift manager's eyes — and oddly enough, even in David's own eyes. Acting in ways that bolster your own integrity actually helps reinforce its value to you.

Adler said that we all strive for superiority, not necessarily the kind that makes us better than our peers (although many competitors really want for that to be true) or that earns us accolades for intellectual or athletic abilities, but for the kind of superiority that makes us happy, satisfied, and content with our lot in life. Striving for superiority means trying to be as competent and effective as we can be. When you make a decision that falls outside of your value system, you are not being true to yourself, and internal emotional conflict will surely result. If your decisions oppose God's will in your life, you are fighting a losing battle.

Abraham Maslow: Self-actualization

Born to Jewish parents who emigrated from Russia, Abraham Maslow was another eminent personality theorist whose ideas still affect current thinking on personality. His theory is often described using a pyramid depicting five levels of needs. From bottom to top, the four lower needs reflect physiological needs such as food, water, shelter, love, and a sense of belonging. The top level, or the fifth level of the pyramid, represents a psychological need Maslow called self-actualization.

Self-actualization reflects an individual's inner state of satisfaction and contentment with who he or she is. Maslow believed that the self-actualized person can be spontaneous, creative, and well connected to others. The self-actualized person has an internalized sense of morality — knowing what is right and wrong without being influenced by outside factors. If integrity is questionable, then that person has probably not reached self-actualization. For them, needs are likely still on a superficial level. They haven't yet internalized the value of personal character and integrity, and all they represent.

Do you remember the movie *Jerry Maguire* where Cuba Gooding Jr., as the athlete Rod Tidwell, introduced the phrase "Show me the money!" to popular culture? He bellowed the phrase whenever he would see his sports agent, Jerry Maguire (played by Tom Cruise), reminding Maguire to find a football contract that would pay big bucks. Money is what Rod Tidwell was all about.

Maslow would probably say that Rod Tidwell wasn't self-actualized because he focused on money and how money helped him feel content. It gave him a sense of identity and security — not self-actualization. We've all laughed at the "Show me the money!" quote and have probably even used it jokingly ourselves. But greed may be one of the biggest factors that keeps any of us from experiencing self-actualization.

People love money. Phrases like, *Put your money where your mouth is, Money talks,* or *Money makes the world go 'round* may be clichés, but they still hold a lot of truth. Money can be an incentive to make a bad choice, tempting us to make decisions that cause us to stray from what we know is right. God says the love of money is the root of all kinds of evil. "Some people, craving money, have wandered from the true faith and pierced themselves with many sorrows (1 Timothy 6:10, NLT).

I'm not saying those who have financial wealth can't be

self-actualized; I am saying that people who have enough money — yet still want more — haven't made it to the top of Maslow's pyramid.

Marcus had an MBA and was a consultant with a software corporation for a little over four years. His older brother, James, was president of his own thriving start-up company, made successful due to James's hard work and a little luck. While growing up in Seattle, the two brothers had always been rivals. Although Marcus was financially successful, he knew he wouldn't be satisfied until he had more financial resources than his brother. In the course of his business travels, Marcus was approached by a colleague at a firm on the West Coast about a venture that, according to his colleague, could supplement his income. The venture would require Marcus to invest money — money he didn't have.

Marcus already had a nice lifestyle. He owned a condo in Magnolia, an upper-end neighborhood in Seattle, and was a season ticketholder for the Seahawks' home games. But he envied his brother's wealth. So Marcus took the lead of his colleague, borrowed money against his condo to access some cash, and dove headfirst into a complex business situation replete with legal problems, sleepless nights, and empty promises. The project quickly went belly-up and so did Marcus's financial status. After losing vast sums of money, Marcus realized his goal had not been to be satisfied financially, but to be better than his brother. No matter how it adds up, money never buys personal satisfaction or self-actualization.

Some Decisions Create Legacies
Honus Wagner, a member of the National Baseball Hall of Fame's inaugural class of 1936, made a decision based on his own values, and he didn't look back. Nearly thirty years prior to his induction

into the Hall of Fame, Honus demanded that the American Tobacco Company take his baseball card out of production. The small, rectangular baseball card had been inserted in cigarette packages, which could get into the hands of children who collected baseball cards. Wagner was adamant: He did not want his likeness used to influence young people to smoke. His decision was final.

Today, because of Wagner's decision to risk his reputation during a time when professional athletes had little bargaining power, Wagner's rare card in great condition easily fetches a collector's bid of over two million dollars. Every time his card is sold, the story of Wagner's decision making and character is told. Ethical decisions do last longer than a lifetime.

A half century later, another baseball icon made a decision that reflected his character. In her book, *Sandy Koufax: A Lefty's Legacy*, Jane Leavy describes how Los Angeles Dodger Sandy Koufax's popularity among Jews and Christians alike soared when he refused to play in the opening game of the 1965 World Series because it was also Yom Kippur, a Jewish holiday set aside for atonement. Historically, Jews don't work on Yom Kippur. By opting to not work at the ballpark that day, Sandy wanted to send the message that Jews should be proud of their heritage. The Dodgers lost game one of the series. But Sandy's character won a much bigger prize, for which he's been recognized for decades.

Another character-based decision made by Branch Rickey in 1945 changed the face of baseball permanently. Rickey, the general manager of the Brooklyn Dodgers, broke racial barriers when he announced that he would sign Jackie Robinson to a contract. Rickey was a successful businessman, a Methodist, and a Republican. He believed that skin color should no longer matter in society.

Not only was Branch Rickey criticized about the racial component of his decision, he was also accused of grandstanding young Robinson just to make money. Rickey had to stand firmly for what he believed to be right, not only for himself but for someone else too. The Robinson-Rickey story reflects the character-based decision of two men who stepped across a boundary together because it was the right move to make.

More Things to Know about Good Decision Making

Every day you make decisions that affect your future. In order to maintain your competitive edge, you need to navigate the decision-making process to the best of your ability. A few simple steps can help you do just that.

Correct bad decisions before they get worse

In a poorly devised plan to run in the Boston Marathon, Rosie Ruiz made a decision and stuck with it, only to look very unintelligent at best. In 1980 Rosie crossed the finish line first in the women's division. She was presented with the green laurel wreath and ceremoniously positioned on the winner's platform in traditional marathon style.

The next day, as officials reviewed the race films, Rosie could not be found anywhere in the footage. Her absence raised suspicion about her legitimacy as the winner. Several members of the marathon audience also came forth saying they had seen Rosie join the marathon only a short distance from the finish line.

Some believe Rosie faked the win to impress her New York employer, who believed she was a great runner. Others suggest that perhaps she did not know which stage of the race she was joining and jumped in too early. Then once she crossed the finish line as the winner, she had to keep up the charade. Although Boston Marathon officials stripped Rosie of her title a week later, to this day Rosie refuses to return her first-place medal.

Whatever the reason, Rosie Ruiz's poor decision to cheat was only made worse when she chose to continue the facade and accept the winner's medal.

Learn to be right-minded rather than always right

Don't confuse the idea of making a right decision with the need to be right all of the time. There is a difference between *knowing the right thing to do* and *being a know-it-all*.

Sammi, a floral designer and mother of two, told me she was tired of nagging her husband, Ben, a sports management consultant, to help with chores around the house. She got upset when he didn't take out the garbage on time, when he left his gym socks strewn about the house, or when he cut the grass only after it was tall enough to stall the mower. In spite of her nagging, none of Ben's behaviors ever seemed to change. The more Sammi protested, the less motivated Ben was to help out. He always had good excuses, believing he was right in his decisions regarding household tasks. In Ben's mind, the garbage didn't need to be taken out until it was full, his socks were always right where he could find them, and mowing the grass aggravated his allergies.

Both Ben and Sammi were right, but each was so determined to be right that they were never able to accomplish anything. Sammi was right in her belief that Ben could help out more. Ben was right in realizing that his reasoning was legitimate. Ironically, being right didn't actually help either of them.

Sammi and Ben realized that they each had their own philosophies about how chores should be done. I suggested to Sammi that she not challenge Ben for a week to see what would happen. She came back to the next session noticeably happier and able to feel better about herself because she had let her self-described nagging go. She noticed that Ben wasn't so defensive around her either. He had even begun picking up his clothes and working in the yard more. Simply put, both Sammi and Ben had wrapped their identities up in being right, not to mention never budging on their positions when they were under attack by the other. Once they learned to let go of their need to be right, they were able to move forward as a team.

Being right does not prove you have character and integrity. In fact, when you are constantly trying to prove that you're right to others, they may begin to see you as uncooperative, insensitive, or demanding.

Some of society's rules leave little room for being wrong. Have you noticed? Doctors must diagnose their patients' illnesses accurately, or they can be sued. Stockbrokers must choose the best stocks, or their clients will take their portfolios elsewhere. Kids have to do well on math, science, and writing tests in order to get into the best colleges. Judges must pass down fair decisions, or they will be harshly criticized in the media.

The personal need to be right about our decisions can be strong. I've talked with many people like Sammi and Ben who are tired of defending themselves all of the time. We simply can't please everyone all of the time, but neither should we set a standard that requires us to be right all of the time. The need to be right will cause problems, first in our close relationships, and then in our work or with teammates. As you learn to make decisions, relieve yourself of this pressure to be "right" by realizing that some problems have more than one good solution.

Use stubbornness to your advantage

Sammi and Ben probably both assumed the other person was more stubborn. But stubbornness may not be such a bad thing under the right circumstances. In fact, stubbornness could be perceived as strong will and determination, which are positive personality characteristics and can be highly desirable in competitors.

Stephanie had been on a Division I college tennis team for two years. During a feedback session at the beginning of her junior season, Stephanie's coach told her that although her spirit and attitude were helpful to the team's morale, she would never be competitive in the conference they competed in. Stephanie was disappointed and angry about the feedback. While she was glad her coach appreciated her work ethic and positive outlook, she was upset that he seemed to have given up on developing her tennis skills.

Stephanie had always had trouble hearing the word "no" when it came to matters of personal development. She decided to disregard her coach's comments and work toward improving her tennis game even though her coach thought she had hit a plateau. Her stubbornness translated to determination and led her to add six more hours a week to her practice routine. She focused on agility, stamina, and biomechanics. As the season continued, Stephanie's coach did notice an improvement. Stubbornness paid off for Stephanie because she made the decision to improve and then stuck with it until it happened.

As you can see, when it comes to integrity, stubbornness can actually be an asset. When the culture in which you compete consistently bombards you with values different from your own, stubbornness helps you to stand firm. Even if everyone around you believes that jeopardizing your character for the win is acceptable, stubbornness can keep you from giving in to that temptation.

Decision Making Made Simple

When faced with difficult decisions that involve your character and integrity, it's a good idea to use some basic strategies to guide your thought process. Let's consider some of them.

Create a pro and con list

Just about everyone knows how to make a pro and con list to help them make a tough decision. In fact, in my clinical practice, I've only had a couple of cases in which I have had to show someone how to make two columns on a sheet of paper, label one column "pro" and the other "con." Everyone has access to this great decision-making tool. Surprisingly, however, even though many people know how to make this list, only a small percentage seem to actually do it. Many people intellectually understand the process of a pro and con list, but they somehow think it happens with no effort. You may know what it's like to change the oil in your vehicle, but until you actually do it, the oil remains unchanged.

To borrow a phrase often used in goal setting, "Don't just think it, ink it." Write down the pros and cons of a tough decision on a piece of paper. The pros column will be easy to fill in. If you're considering a job transition, for example, more money, better medical benefits, more respect from colleagues, more vacation, IRA matching, and tuition reimbursement might go into the pros column. The cons column might be more difficult to complete; it's actually a good thing. If nothing shows up in the cons column, your decision will be easy to make. But if a factor that contradicts your values — exploitation of junior staff, use of undesignated funds for personal time, less accountability about time honestly worked — makes the list, the decision should probably — maybe even definitely — be no.

Gather information

Too often when we have a decision to make, we move forward before gathering enough information. Relying solely on personal knowledge is insufficient. Other sources of information abound; you simply have to know where to look. Gather facts and opinions from friends, family, and experts. Research as many factors as you can about your decision. Solicit information from sources that may offer a different perspective than your personal experiences. You need to make a good decision, so you'll need all the information you can get.

Shannon had been offered a nursing position by a physician in a midsized city. She was excited about it because she wanted to work in a family practice. Although she had been told about her salary, benefits, vacation, and scheduling, she knew she needed more details before making her decision. Shannon decided to ask friends and neighbors about the doctor's reputation and clinic. She had an old friend from nursing school who had worked in the practice many years ago. Shannon gave her a call too. After a brief telephone visit, Shannon learned that the work environment in the practice was lacking. The physician was known to charge for unnecessary medical procedures and his treatment of women in the office was also questionable. Shannon called a few former employees of the practice, learning more each time about the dwindling integrity of the physician. She was disappointed with the news, but she was glad to have found out ahead of time. This information was crucial for Shannon as she made her decision to wait for another job opportunity in the type of practice she desired.

Get creative with your options

When making a decision, we tend think of options in sets of two. For example, do I take the job or do I stay where I am, do I buy a new car or a used car, do I invest in this stock or in that stock? Do you see how this works? Having more than two options to choose from can make decision making easier.

Consider Dan. Dan is thinking about dating a woman in his office, even though they have little in common and even seem to share dissimilar values. Dan thinks he has two options: date this woman or don't date her. He may, however, be overlooking several other choices. He could spend time getting to know her through e-mail conversations, join her in social groups, invite a friend to join them both for lunch, or simply talk with her on the phone if she is willing. These are all ways of connecting relationally before deciding to pursue a romance. Thinking outside of the box in order to create possible solutions will give Dan far more options than simply dating this woman or not dating her. Maybe she'll have a few suggestions too.

Recognize the Right Decision and Make It

I should have expected that right in the middle of writing this book, I'd be confronted with a decision that could reflect on my character. It was one of those situations that nobody would ever know about — or even care about — but it would put a price tag on my character.

I was traveling and found a tweed blazer in a store that I really liked. Of course, the store only had the size smaller and two sizes larger than what I needed. The clerk told me that with some minor alterations, the jacket would fit perfectly. Even better, the jacket was nearly a third off of the original price. I hauled the jacket back to Boston and visited the tailor down the street from my house the next day.

The tailor told me she could make the jacket fit, but the pattern in the material wouldn't look right. It would be gathered and bunched. This sale jacket was getting complicated. I took the jacket to another tailor a few blocks over for a second opinion. He agreed with the first tailor. The jacket wasn't meant to be worn by me.

I called the store where I bought what was now the tweed burden of the year. The store manager said that the simplest solution was for them to order a jacket in the correct size and ship it to me. I could take the original jacket to a sister store in Boston and get a refund. The store manager even honored the sale price on the second jacket and it arrived within days—but it didn't fit either. Now I owned two jackets, neither of which fit. I had grown sick of this jacket. Are you following this story?

I took both jackets back to the sister store. They refunded my money for the first jacket because I had a receipt, but I had no receipt for the second jacket (that cost the same price as the first one, which was on sale.) The clerk said that without a receipt she could only give me a store credit for the original price of the second jacket, even though she had just refunded me the sale price for the first jacket.

She gave me a gift card for the full amount of the jacket—not the sale price—which was more than what I had paid. Now you see my dilemma. A price tag had just been put on my character. Would I sell it? I'm not telling you this story so I can sound like a saint. I'm telling you because I struggled with this decision just like everyone who struggles with integrity decisions. It would have been so easy to justify keeping the higher amount because of all the trouble I had gone through. My internal rationalizations sounded something like this: *The first clerk sold me a jacket that wouldn't fit. I traveled to two tailors and was now dealing with another clerk who really doesn't want to accept a returned sale item — let alone two of them. For a couple of weeks, I've been out the cash on two jackets that I didn't even need.*

The rationalization for keeping the extra cash was there, but I still knew I had gotten back more money than I should have.

I explained to the clerk that by not having a receipt I was actually making money off of her store. The clerk seemed puzzled — maybe even annoyed — that I had even raised the issue. She told me she had to follow the store policy and not all of their policies made sense. She thanked me for my honesty but said it was really no big deal to her company, because such an insignificant amount of money wasn't worth trying to resolve. After I left the store, I realized that my character had actually earned a little money that day. For the clerk, my integrity was no big deal, but for me its value had just increased.

In order to defend your character, you've got to be able to make the right decision and not look back. The athletic training motto, "No pain, no gain" may even be appropriate in such cases. Don't be surprised to find that decisions that reflect values are often unpopular, criticized, or mocked. Making the right decision, and then acting on it, is one of the best ways of demonstrating your character when you compete.

POSTGAME REVIEW

× Decide the value of your character and integrity.

× Ask yourself, *At what price would I sell my character and integrity?*

× Give your character a voice. Speak up for your values.

× Consider what motivates your decisions. Is it integrity?

× Be willing to correct a bad decision.

× Learn that *trying* to be right doesn't *make* you right.

× Realize your decisions create a legacy that can last much longer than you.

× Use decision-making strategies like a pro and con list, gathering detailed information or creating additional solutions to your problem.

PRINCIPLE 3

Define Goals That
Reflect Your Values

*If you set a goal for yourself and are able to achieve it, you have
won your race. Your goal can be to come in first, to improve
your performance, or just finish the race — it's up to you."*

Dave Scott
First Ironman Hall of Fame inductee

According to founding father Alexander Hamilton, if we don't stand
for something, we'll fall for anything. Those words couldn't be any
more true for individuals who are interested in living a life of integrity and character. We must know what it is that we're striving for in
life so that we don't settle for something that reflects our character
poorly. And the key to striving for integrity is having well-defined
goals. Setting goals can be a challenging task, but with some understanding of basic goal-setting strategies, you will be heading yourself in the right direction.

Nancy was a forty-eight-year-old marathon runner I met in the
medical tent when her doctor called me in for a psychological con-
sultation. When I saw Nancy the first time, she was lying on her cot,
sobbing uncontrollably. She had been unresponsive to the supportive clinicians trying to help her.

Rather than saying much, I told Nancy I was going to hold

her hand in mine and we could communicate by squeezing hands since her emotions weren't allowing her to talk at that moment. One squeeze would be yes. Two would be no. I asked her to squeeze my hand once if it was comfortable for her to communicate this way for a little while. If she didn't squeeze at all, I would know she wasn't interested in communicating with me. She squeezed. I asked her if she was having any physical pain. She squeezed twice. I then said that the goal for her running must have been very important to her. She squeezed my hand once and continued to cry. I said that whatever her goal for running was, it was clearly very personal. She squeezed one hard squeeze.

I began to narrow the types of feelings in order to understand how I could help her. She squeezed twice when I asked if she was feeling sad, disappointed, angry, confused, or anxious. I asked about positive feelings that Nancy started endorsing with her single squeezes. She squeezed the hardest when I asked if she felt relieved. She didn't look relieved.

> *Those who stand for nothing fall for anything.*
> Alexander Hamilton
> American founding father

I offered Nancy some strategies for regaining her composure, including breathing exercises and some easy visual imagery. These were exercises she could use without having to talk. She took me up on the offer and began to look more relaxed. In only a few minutes of relaxing, she was able to talk to me about her goal for running the marathon. I had paid such close attention to Nancy's squeezes that I hadn't noticed she was wearing two thin, gold wedding bands on her left hand. They had belonged to her parents, both of whom had died within the last year from different terminal illnesses.

Nancy had decided to run the marathon as a way of honoring her parents, but she wasn't prepared for the emotional experience she would have. For Nancy, the marathon was a metaphor for her parents' battles with their diseases. Nancy noticed as she came closer to the finish line, it became more difficult to run. She had minimal energy. Her physical pain grew with each labored step. She thought that she must be paralleling the experience her parents had had with their illnesses: Close to the end of their lives, it had become more physically difficult for them to go on.

Nancy had wanted to honor her parents by finishing the race. Finish she did—in a way that certainly honored her parents and reflected her character. And when Nancy crossed the finish line and achieved her goal, she was simply overwhelmed with great relief.

Necessary Ingredients for Good Goals

Goal setting is basic to sports, business, and life. By setting reasonable goals and keeping your focus on them, not only can you achieve greater success—you can reach your goals while keeping your character intact.

Whether in athletics or business, goals vary in shape, size, importance, and meaning. They may not be well-defined goals, but they are goals nonetheless. For swimmers, the goal is the fastest time. In marketing, the goal is name recognition. In sales, it's about closing the deal. In fencing, the goal is scoring touches. In golf, the goal is to be under par. In graduate school, it's all about the GPA.

As a clinical sport psychologist, I frequently work in locker rooms or on the court rather than in my office. One scorching afternoon, I had a session with a minor-league baseball player named Rodney while we played a rhythmic game of catch in the freshly mowed outfield grass. I can still hear the occasional pop of the ball hitting our gloves and echoing off of the tall wooden fence that traced the warning track. As we played catch, we discussed Rodney's goals. Even though he was an outstanding player, he didn't have any idea about how to set a goal he could reach. Our conversation went something like this:

"I'm glad you decided to call me. How do you think I can help you out? What's your goal?"

"I just want to improve. I need to be better."

"Tell me what *better* means to you."

"I just need to be better. I know I can do better, and I won't be satisfied with myself until I do the very best that I know I can do."

"I hear what you're saying. What are the stats from last year that you want to improve?"

"I led the team in doubles and triples . . . ended up with the third best batting average in the league before going into the play-offs."

"It sounds to me like you're hitting well. Are you sure you need to improve your hitting or should you just maintain your performance from last year?"

"If I don't do better than last year, I won't be happy about my performance."

"How are you planning to know if you have improved from last year?"

"Oh, I'll just know because I'll get a feeling that I've improved."

My conversation with Rodney in the outfield was similar to many conversations I have with clients. People generally want to change behavior, but they make a crucial error by not setting goals to measure personal progress. Too often, clients want to set goals based on a *feeling* or *sense* that something has improved. By contrast, a good goal is both observable and measurable. In order to understand how to set a goal and reach it consistently, you must first know the difference between two types of common, yet important, goals: outcome goals and performance goals.

Goals should be based on performance rather than outcome

Outcome goals describe the status of the game at the very end of competition. They are only useful for defining who won and who lost and never provide a good representation of the performance before the outcome occurs — what actually happened during a game. Winning a game is an outcome goal.

Local sportscasters often begin a story with announcing the winning score — the outcome goal — before rewinding to review the highlights of the game. You've seen the reports I'm describing. Some unsuspecting coach gets doused with a water jug and players pick him up to parade him before a wildly cheering crowd of fans. Then the sportscaster goes back to review all of the important plays that led up to the victory. While outcome goals can be important goals, we often focus too much attention on them, which can leave us feeling negatively about our performance if we lose.

> *Set your goals high, and don't stop till you get there.*
> Bo Jackson
> 1985 Heisman Trophy winner
> &
> 1989 MLB All-Star game MVP

Rodney saw me for psychological skills training to improve his hitting. As I was getting to know him, I asked Rodney to tell me about times when he wasn't hitting well. He described a game in which he had walked once and hit two singles, a double, and a sacrifice fly. During that same game, a couple of his teammates struck out, and one of those teammates also made a bad base-running error. That error cost them the game.

Rather than considering his individual batting performance, Rodney based his effectiveness as a hitter on the outcome goal of winning or losing the game. This perspective was a dangerous way for Rodney to evaluate himself, because he let something outside of his own actions and control determine how he felt about his performance. He wasn't happy.

Sometimes people like Rodney are so focused on outcome goals that they are willing to compromise character in order to be more successful. While Rodney resisted the appeal of performance-enhancing drugs or using an illegal bat, he frequently dealt with anger, disappointment, and self-doubt. His negative thoughts and emotions defined him until he became acquainted with a healthier type of goal called a performance goal.

Performance goals are goals based on one's prior personal performances. They allow an athlete to better control steps leading to success because these goals aren't determined by box scores, but by individual improvements.

Rodney's self-critical style faded as soon as he began setting and achieving performance goals rather than outcome goals. At the beginning of each week, he set performance goals such as keeping his batting average equal to or higher than the previous week and hitting a single each game. He tried to limit his fielding errors to no more than one every two weeks. By moving his focus from the outcome goal of winning to the performance goal of personal improvement, Rodney was able to achieve his goals and become a better ballplayer. His confidence increased and his satisfaction with his performance continued to strengthen regardless of his team's overall win-loss record.

Performance goals, sometimes referred to as process goals, are helpful in preparation too. Rodney realized he could apply performance goal strategies to his practice and workout schedule as well. In order to hit a single during each game, he knew certain training requirements should be met each week. Rodney decided he needed to run ten miles each week, visually track at least one hundred pitches in the hitting tunnel every day, and spend fifteen minutes daily reviewing scouting reports of pitchers he would face during the upcoming games. For Rodney, reaching each of these goals would lead him to achieve other performance goals. And by attaining his performance goals, Rodney increased the likelihood that he would also achieve his outcome goal: winning the game.

Goals should be observable and objective

While most of us want to improve at what we do, "doing better" isn't really observable. Remember, Rodney wanted to improve his hitting and become a more complete ballplayer. But his fans wouldn't be able to say to each other, "Wow. Did you just see Rodney do better?" Rodney said for him, doing better would be based on a feeling he would have. But we can't really see Rodney's feelings. Rodney needed to make his goals observable.

One way of making sure goals are observable is to ask yourself this question: "If fifty people saw my performance, would they all agree they saw me do the same thing?" If the answer is yes, you've identified an observable goal. Rodney's feelings and thoughts couldn't be observed. But fifty of his fans could all agree they saw him hit a double or a triple, because doubles and triples are observable. Anyone watching can see it happen.

Once an observable goal is defined, a way of measuring it should be put in place. Goals can be measured by various methods including time, frequency, percentages, or averages. Rodney wanted to hit one single each game and decrease the frequency of his strikeouts compared to last season. These goals are observable and measurable. If goals aren't measurable, it's difficult to know to what extent behavior change has occurred or if it has at all. Objective goals are goals that can be counted in discrete terms, like quantity or frequency.

Another effective strategy for identifying objective goals is to think of goals as you would landmarks. Landmarks are easy to recognize. For example, if your goal is to take a trip to Hollywood, objective measures that you would use to determine you've met your goal would include seeing the huge Hollywood sign, leafy palm trees, historic Grauman's Chinese Theater, and the Hollywood Walk of Fame. If instead, you saw the soaring Space Needle, Mount Rainier in the distance, and lively Pike Place Market, you would know your goal of taking a trip to Hollywood had gone south—or north, as it were. You hadn't made it to Hollywood, but to Seattle.

Goals should be the right size

When setting goals, the old restaurant buffet phenomenon can easily occur: Our eyes can be bigger than our stomachs. It's a common mistake to take on a project you just don't have the time, resources, or skill to see through. On the other hand, a goal that doesn't require much effort or skill can end up in the unachieved goals category too.

Finding a goal that is challenging and is within your personal reach is best for maintaining your interest and energizing you. But if the goal isn't a good fit, you could find yourself in a situation where character and integrity can be compromised. You may be tempted to cut corners or cheat, just to come close to accomplishing what you had set out to do.

Have you ever started a project with the intention of attaining a specific outcome, but the farther along you got in your efforts the less recognizable the outcome became? Maybe the twenty pounds of muscle you wanted to build turned out to be only five, or the amazing speed you wanted to be known for on the court was noticed by everyone else as nothing more than old-fashioned hustle. Maybe the vast profit margins you convinced yourself that you could generate were seen by your supervisor as only a good effort on which to build next year's gains. It can be pretty disappointing.

You may ask yourself what you did wrong. You thought you had a reasonable goal but somehow it didn't unfold according to plan. Maybe the resources weren't there, you didn't have enough help, or you ran out of time. Maybe somewhere along the way, you settled for something less than what your head and heart knew to be best. Why do we sometimes fail to reach our goals, maybe even missing them by a long shot? Well, we're simply aiming for the wrong goal.

A new football coach had accepted a head coaching position at a junior college. He knew that as the new kid on the block, his reputation was being shaped by the performance of his team. He believed he deserved the respect of the college, the community, and his players, and he was convinced a perfect season would be just what was needed to give him the status he wanted so desperately.

During the first team meeting, he told his players that his plan was for them to be undefeated this season. After losing all twelve of the previous season's scheduled games, this was a tough goal for many of the players to even consider. Some immediately began to feel hopeless, and a couple of seniors even quit the team after the meeting. But even though his goal for the team didn't seem to be within their reach, the coach remained enthusiastic about meeting it.

Somehow, the team won their first two games by a scant margin and a few bad calls. The coach was energized by the two wins and began to put even more pressure on the players to have an undefeated season. In order to do that, some of the players decided they needed new strategies for improving their game. They started skipping classes so they could lift weights in the weight room. And several players began a new supplement diet in order to increase their overall body mass. With his focus only on the outcome goal of an undefeated season, the coach overlooked the fact that his players weren't attending classes and were possibly harming themselves with supplements. He told them that he liked their dedication to winning. As you can recognize, the coach's poorly chosen goals caused him and his players to undermine their own personal integrity and develop a win-at-all-costs attitude.

In this case, the coach set goals too high for himself. His ego became involved and he projected those terrible goals onto his team. There wouldn't have been anything wrong with setting a goal to win games. But wanting to win *all* of them was simply not within the current team's ability. The coach could have considered other reasonable goals for his team. He could have had more success his first year by setting goals such as winning four games or increasing the number of players on the team. But because the goals were out of reach, integrity was compromised. The team won two more games, which would have been a considerable improvement over last season. Unfortunately, the coach and team focused more on the eight losses they had. As a result, the football program took a dive the following year.

Strategies for Achieving Your Goals

Once you've learned how to set achievable goals, you need some practical strategies for attaining them. Consider implementing some of the following ideas in your quest for success.

Put it in writing

Once you select a goal for yourself, writing it down can be an effective way of consolidating that goal and making it realistic. Oftentimes, people write their goals on a piece of paper and then post it in a place where they will see it frequently.

Some of my clients have written down their goals in creative ways. Mario, a financial consultant, wrote his goal on a card and then mailed it to his wife. Janis, a medical resident, penned her goal on a prescription pad with the words "Doctor's Orders" above it. Veronica, a real estate agent, wrote her goal in her PDA and programmed it to repeat daily so she would read it every time she looked at her schedule. A college wrestler named Chad saved his goal in a special file on his computer at the beginning of each week and printed it out, folded it, and put it under his pillow. He read it before going to sleep every night and then again when he awoke the next morning. Sam, a head football coach, wrote his goal on an opponent's jersey and then nailed it to his office door in the locker room.

Goals that exist both inside and outside of a competitor's head won't easily be forgotten.

Create a fan club

Once you've chosen and defined your goals, let others know about them. You can begin building a team that includes family, close friends, and coworkers who will provide unique ways of supporting your goals and encouraging you. Your fans might be friends from college, a trusted professor or business manager, your spouse, therapist, siblings, parents, or minister. Choose such people wisely. You can also share your goals with God, who wants to help you meet them (Psalm 37:4).

All of these sources of goal support can offer accountability, encouragement, and celebration. Each person plays a different role in your life, so the support each person can offer is unique because of the individual relationship he or she has with you.

When I'm working with the Boston Marathon medical team, I have the opportunity to meet runners from across the United States, as well as other countries. Each runner's story about his or her journey to Boston is unique. And yet, while their stories are different, many of them share the same hope of completing the marathon and being changed personally in some way.

Twenty-four-year-old Jonas, a Scandinavian runner, was lying on a cot in the medical tent when we began our conversation. His skin looked very pale; his eyes were reddened and swollen from crying. He had just finished the marathon but missed his personal best time by less than ten minutes. As we talked, he admitted his disappointment in what seemed to me to be a good time for running the marathon. He went on to tell me that more than being disappointed about his time, he was embarrassed to tell his friends at home he had not met his personal goal.

As I listened, he told me his friends and he frequently compete in many areas of their lives including athletics, business, dating, and finances. At least once a week, they go out for dinner and talk about their accomplishments. They talk as if they are invincible, never complaining about being challenged by the next goal. It's expected that once one of them reaches a goal, a new, more difficult goal is set. He looked at me with his tear-filled eyes, and said, "This isn't just about me not making my time today, is it? It's about me having confidence in myself and what I'm capable of doing. This way of thinking isn't just in my marathon training, but at work and with my buddies. I need to learn to be satisfied with myself. I'm good enough, aren't I?"

I wish every session I had with a client ran as smoothly as my brief chat with Jonas. He was right. First of all, the support group he had chosen was not one that provided healthy encouragement. But even more, the goals he set for himself caused tremendous stress and didn't help him consolidate any solid positive beliefs about himself. Jonas needed to reevaluate his goals in athletics, business, and relationships in order to find contentment. By aiming for solid, character-based goals, he would be settling for nothing less than that which reflects his very best—a mighty achievement for him.

Be prepared to defend your goals

Like any other goal, character and integrity are often at the center of people's target. They genuinely want to hit that center. However, what they aim for and what they actually hit can be two different targets altogether. Many factors can affect their aim: They take their eyes off of the target, someone distracts them, they get nervous about the outcome of the game, or they simply believe they just can't hit the center perfectly.

The truth is that everyone's aim becomes shaky at times. And if we aren't prepared, it's easy to miss the mark of character and integrity. The apostle Paul was preaching in Thessalonica when he was mobbed by some local folks who didn't like his agenda. In an effort to stand on principle and keep his goal foremost in his mind, Paul pled with them, "We were not preaching with any false motives or evil purposes in mind; we were perfectly straightforward and sincere" (1 Thessalonians 2:3, TLB). Paul understood how important it is to guard against being knocked off an honorable course by dishonest strategies. The Thessalonians wanted to derail Paul and keep him from reaching his goal, but he stood firm. Even today, it's easy to be thrown off course when reaching for our goals.

Anna was a member of a four-person budgetary committee within her corporation. She was pleased to be employed by a company that prioritized character and loyalty over financial gain. She had adopted the very same philosophy before she ever applied for business school, and was excited to work for a company that shared her values.

The committee had been organized with the sole purpose of executing a business plan that would lead to the production of a new piece of laboratory equipment used in the treatment of blood diseases. Anna's company was considered altruistic and frequently spent money to provide medical care in developing countries where newer treatments were not readily available. Anna, along with the other committee members, was responsible for securing contracts with vendors who would play important roles in the development of the equipment and do it for minimal expense. So far, so good. The business mission itself was even aligned with Anna's values.

Anna decided to accept a bid from a small plastics company that made an important piece of the equipment her team was engineering. She met with the owner of the company several times, finally agreed on the finances, and then discussed logistics related to shipping and production deadlines. They both signed the contract and hoped to begin production in four months.

A week later, Anna participated in a routine business meeting with her planning team. During the meeting, one of her coworkers said he had recently received a lower bid for the plastics contract from another company that had failed to meet the bid deadline. The coworker thought that even though an agreement with the first company was already in place, the team's attorney could find a loophole in the contract so the committee could work with the least expensive company. The suggestion made by her team member put Anna in an integrity bind.

Many people in Anna's situation would use the loophole, secure the cheaper contract, and call it a "business decision." Anna could even justify it by pointing to the greater good of the ends they were trying to achieve: delivering cost-effective treatments to the third world.

But Anna understood the importance of living by her word. As Jesus' words, "let your 'yes' be 'yes,'" echoed in her mind, she thought about the relationship she had developed with the owner of the plastics company. If she changed her decision, that owner would have no faith in Anna's business practices and might even tell other businesses in the industry about his bad experience with her. Her character was on the line.

Anna's brave response to her team included an interesting spin. She conveyed her concern about how the plastics company owner would likely respond to her breaking the contract and how that would potentially affect their market image. But more importantly, she asserted with courage, "I wish this vendor had bid on time. However, since he didn't, I would let each of you on the committee down if I didn't keep my word with the man I've agreed to work with. You rely on me to make sound decisions. Making a decision that compromises the validity of my word could cause you to question my motives and reliability on other projects in the future. There is more at stake than just a small amount of money that is relatively insignificant."

The contract remained in place and the plastics owner never knew any different. Anna had kept her focus on her goal: maintaining her integrity in the way she practiced business. Her goal was to stand firmly on values, and she achieved it. Her decision was critical for helping the team gain clearer vision for a project that could have easily been blurred by loopholes and double-talk.

Find the "I" (integrity) in team

What happens when a team or work group doesn't really care about the quality of integrity as long as the goal appears to be reached? It can be tempting, as the cliché goes, to fake it as if you've made it. Values, integrity, and character are commonly sacrificed in the name of accomplishment, especially in today's culture. Teams don't put genuine effort into their practices. Meetings are cut short. Monthly reports and training seminars are fabricated so senior management will think progress is being made toward a goal.

The group can easily find ways to justify its actions: *Management is out of touch; These goals were always unrealistic; or They won't listen to us anyway when we tell them they're off base.* This justification, pointing fingers at those who "make" them lie or cut corners, is used to put the blame on someone else for a group's lack of integrity.

When you are the only one with integrity on your team, it's easy to feel as if you're lost in an ethical wilderness without a moral compass. The people around you are navigating by a different map, and you will need true landmarks in order to find your way out. If you aren't focused on a specific goal as your landmark, your teammates, coworkers, and competitors can easily undermine your integrity.

In order to protect your values, you must define and remain focused on the goals that reflect them. Just like Anna, who cleared up the murky waters of integrity in her team's business deal, you can stand firmly on your values.

If you are part of a team that is struggling with the temptation to compromise for the sake of a goal, the following strategies might be helpful:

1. Respectfully point out to the team that the goals of the team seem to have shifted.

2. Seek outside support from mentors and colleagues who can help you stay focused on goals and affirm the dilemma that you face.

3. Increase communication with team members so motives and goals are clear.

4. As a last possible resort, withdraw from the team rather than compromise your character.

When There's a Will, There's a Goal

Prior to the Boston Marathon, the local convention center hosts a sports and fitness expo, which features the latest developments in running technology, athletic nutrition, marathon souvenirs, injury prevention strategies, and personalized memorabilia. Thousands of runners, families, and friends wind through the aisles of interactive booths, many of which offer samples and hint at an unspoken advantage if their products are used. In this energized atmosphere, die-hard runners may even recognize legendary marathoners mixing with the crowds of people.

At a recent expo, Adidas built the Reasons to Run wall. The wall had thousands of miniature marathon bibs printed on it. Bibs are individually numbered and worn by each official marathon runner. For the Boston Marathon, over fifteen thousand bibs are given to runners each year.

Whether a runner's number was 2,157 or 15,823, it was on the Reasons to Run wall. Runners were expected to use the blank space on the wall by their bib number to write the reasons they were running the marathon. While many exhibits at the expo were interesting, this wall created a noticeable buzz. Crowds of people enjoyed the chance to peer into someone's private life and learn what motivated them to run such a grueling race.

The wall affirmed the personal experiences of runners and served as a reminder for everyone about how goals and motivations have unique meanings. While people gave thousands of reasons to run, I jotted down some that really seemed to stand out. Here are some that caught my eye.

"Third time is a charm."
"I can do all things through Christ."
"In memory of my dad."
"Good-bye 2006. Hello to finishing this year!"
"I needed a vacation."

"For my kids, Emma and Ethan."

"Swimsuit season!"

"I run because I need alone time."

"The road is my therapist."

"Because my wife thinks runners are sexy."

"I feel immortal when I run."

"Because my family makes me do it."

"It's always been my dream to run Boston."

"My students inspire me to be the best I can be."

"In honor of my dog Smokey."

"I thrive on pain."

"To test my personal limits."

"Because I still can run at age 83."

"Because God blessed me with two strong legs."

"Because chicks dig it."

"Because chubby and Speedo don't mix."

"Because I'm a psycho."

While a few of the reasons listed were humorous, many reflected values including relationships, spirituality, and personal improvement. The wall is a good example of how values can correspond with a goal. You may need to ask yourself why you do what you do and how your values are connected to your goals. What motivates you to work toward your goal? To what length will you go to meet your goal?

Goals that reflect integrity and character are goals that you achieve by utilizing your own resources. When you achieve these goals, you can be satisfied that you reached deep within yourself to get the job done right.

POSTGAME REVIEW

✗ Define goals that are objective and measurable.
✗ Write down your goals.
✗ Share your goals with others.
✗ Create a fan club of supporters who can encourage you.
✗ Understand that outcome goals may not represent your performance well.
✗ Use performance goals to determine your own abilities and progress.
✗ Make sure your goal is reasonable—not too easy, not too difficult.
✗ Clarify the personal and powerful reasons you reach for a goal.

PRINCIPLE 4

Rethink Winning

Winning isn't everything — but wanting to win is.

Vince Lombardi
Legendary NFL coach

Several years ago when I was a psychology intern in Louisiana, I decided to run a 5K race at a local Air Force base. The race was one of those "under the stars" fun runs set to begin after the humid Louisiana temperatures dropped in the evening. I drove to England Air Force Base, put on my glow-in-the-dark participant T-shirt, and resolutely began my stretching. My performance goal for the race was simply to finish.

The start of the race came and went, and I was off to meet my goal of completing five kilometers. I paced myself and used some sport psychology strategies when I needed them. After crossing the finish line, I grabbed my complimentary bottle of water and made my way to the table where I had been instructed to check in with the official to receive my finishing time.

I was surprised to learn that I might have finished first in my age division. But she told me another timekeeper was also logging time for other runners and to check back in twenty minutes. I wandered around to kill some time. My goal of completing the 5K run had suddenly transformed into a glimmering hope of winning my age division. I tried to be patient.

After twenty minutes went by, I checked again with the first official. She said my score still stood as the best time, but she didn't know about the other scorekeeper. She told me to take another twenty-minute break and check back again. Many of the runners had crossed the finish line as I returned again to the timekeeper, rather confidently I might add. She told me that she had submitted her time sheet to the judging table and that I should now go there to learn the final results.

I made my way through the bustle of runners, waited in line, and asked the woman in charge of the table about my ranking. She looked up my name and bib number, then smiled, and congratulated me on having placed first in my division. I couldn't believe it. Was it hidden talent? Was I in better shape than I first thought? Should I consider running more races to develop my speed? What had begun as an evening of exercise had evolved into a small ego boost and novice career in running. Feeling quite stunned and outwardly confident, I asked the woman by what margin I beat second place. She skimmed her list, looked at me over the top of her glasses, and informed me that second place wasn't even close—I was the only runner entered in my age division. She chortled as I picked my run-like-the-wind ego off of the ground.

Winning is just a label, and it can be perfectly meaningless. I can laugh as I share the story with you now, but I remember how quickly my perspective about winning that race changed when the woman broke the news to me. It wasn't as if I had lost a gold medal, but I had learned how quickly—in an instant—perspective can change. It's this human ability to change perspective that can help your character survive in heated competition.

Is it fair to say that if people never won, nobody would ever cheat? The notion may be simplistic, but I believe it is true. Winning, as we saw in the last chapter, is an outcome goal, and it consumes society from infancy through adulthood. Whether it is baby pageants, youth sporting events, art and music contests, sales campaigns, or politics, winning is important. No one wants to be the proverbial rotten egg by being last — or even second place for that matter.

When people place such strong emphasis on winning, however, they are apt to overvalue it and sacrifice integrity for the blue ribbon. And when winning is overvalued, competitors go to rather ridiculous lengths in order to measure up. They spend too much money on the best equipment, enroll in every advanced training seminar they can find, sacrifice family time, and basically become obsessed with their quest for success. The fun is gone.

But it is possible to guard yourself from character-eroding competition. You can preserve your integrity if you learn to rethink winning in personal terms, which will in turn allow you to experience victory more frequently.

As you dive into this chapter, you may be asking yourself this question: Is it even possible to think of winning in any other way than what we know in our culture? Jim Vitti, author of *The Cubs on Catalina* and *The Brooklyn Dodgers in Cuba*, believes that it is. Jim's unique perspective on winning comes from researching and interviewing early-century professional baseball players. Contrasted with the way winners acted several generations ago, winners today often behave very arrogantly. I spoke to Jim about his research, and this is what he told me: "Athletes (even the biggest of the big, like

[Babe] Ruth) simply didn't show up the competition in those days. Guys would even run the bases with their heads down after hitting a homer, for instance, to avoid disrespecting the pitcher and the other team. How stark a contrast to today's power hitters, standing in the box after their blast, and today's end-zone dances in pro football!" The important point Jim draws from his research is that winning, and how it is experienced, has apparently changed shape and appearance over time. We are able to keep winning and the rituals of winning in line with our values.

Our culture shapes what we think about winning. You don't have to say good-bye to ticker-tape parades, champagne bottle hose-downs, or telephone calls from the president. But to compete with character, you will have to broaden your definition of winning to accommodate more than just what culture says about winning.

Think like a Psychologist

Psychologists use a strategy competitors should learn to use as well: reframing. This is a valuable technique for helping an individual see a less desirable situation from a new, positive perspective.

One of my favorite personal examples of reframing came about after my wife and I had become parents for the first time. When we brought Grant home, his crying would wake us up in the middle of the night. My naive reaction was frustration mixed with disorientation, due to the loss of sleep. As most new parents know, responding to every little noise can be an all-night job. But with reframing, I learned to see his cry as my opportunity to rescue him from hunger and get him to his mother fast. Under the cover of darkness, I got to be a bona fide superhero rather than a grumpy dad who's resentful about getting out of bed. Who would ever pass up the chance to be a

hero? I sure didn't. You see how the negative aspect of sleep distur-
bance is shifted to a winning circumstance by reframing it?

There are other instances where reframes are helpful in our lives,
both at work and at home. For example, a boss who wants to know
every detail of an employee's progress could easily be perceived as a
micromanager. But reframed, he may be perceived as offering his full
attention to his employees so they will be successful. The latter explanation is much more appealing. Another example of how reframing
is used is in the example of a husband
who questions his wife's decision to
work late. He could be either a control freak or a spouse who wants the
best for his wife, including time at
home where she can relax from her
hectic work schedule. A coworker
who argues about every decision
could be viewed as a troublemaker
or as a detail-oriented employee. I

> *A good mind
> has never
> handicapped
> a player.*
> Pete Carril
> Former Princeton
> basketball coach

think you probably get the picture. In many situations, reframing
offers a positive perspective on a difficult situation or relationship.
Reframing can also help you find ways of winning more than you
ever have before and at the same time reduce negative feelings such
as envy or jealousy that could provoke you to try to win next time
using dishonest methods.

When we reframe our wins and losses, we strengthen our character. We also learn how to win more frequently and abandon society's
notion that victory should be acquired with an at-all-costs attitude.
Changing ways of thinking can require more than just a psychological
intervention. It has scriptural roots as well. Matthew 20 tells a parable

of a landowner who paid laborers who had worked only a few hours the same wage as those who had sweated in the field all day long. This story shows a completely different perspective on who the real winners were, and it made some of the workers angry. In that case, the last could be first, and the first could be last. That's what we're doing when we reframe. We're finding ways of coming out on top, even when we don't win the grand prize.

If you think that reframing is just a bunch of psychological smoke and mirrors, stop for a moment and consider Romans 8:28 (NLT). This passage offers an encouraging guarantee:

And we know that God causes everything to work together for the good of those who love God and are called according to his purpose for them.

This passage is often cited when some tragedy or bad event happens in someone's life. I've known some athletes who have used it as a way of helping them when their career seemed to have stalled or when life had thrown them a curveball that changed their future. Even if the good isn't immediately recognizable and the win isn't obvious, you can still be a winner because this passage promises that the Lord is at work in your life. You can know that something positive is happening or is going to happen, even if you can't see it. This is truly a reframe.

In addition to the psychological intervention of reframing, additional strategies can help you find satisfaction in your performance, even if the color of your ribbon isn't blue.

Winners Look Good Wearing Gray

Some competitors commit serious thinking errors when it comes to winning. They think of winning in terms of being an all-or-nothing event. Such a label is something like a light switch — it's either on or off — no in-between.

Also called black-and-white thinking, this perception can create serious self-image problems. The notion that you can be 100 percent perfect at anything is a bit hard to believe. You may be 100 percent human, but that's about it. Politicians never receive *all* of the votes from the populace. Bankers don't control *all* of the money in a community. Jockeys don't win *every* race. Kickers don't make *every* goal. My clients usually agree that they need to abandon the notion of black or white and start looking for areas of gray. They find success there every time.

Jack had a reputation for sealing hefty financial deals with corporate clients over lunch. He had gained quite a reputation in his company for being the go-to man when large sums of cash were on the table. Although he was new to the game of negotiation, he had met with impressive success, which developed an outcome-based confidence in Jack. His bank account had grown fast.

In June, just before the close of the fiscal year for his company, Jack was at lunch with new clients he had courted for several months. He intended to enter into an agreement that would set a financial record for his company — and himself. However, at the end of surf, turf, and dessert, Jack's clients opted to hold on to the cash Jack had been eyeing. The close of the fiscal year was occurring for them too; they were over budget.

In spite of his polished ability to negotiate contracts by meeting

> *Let me win, but*
> *if I cannot win,*
> *let me be brave*
> *in the attempt.*
> Special Olympics
> motto

people halfway, Jack was a black-and-white thinker when it came to dealing with himself. Since he didn't win, he saw the outcome of that business dinner as a major loss that reflected his weaknesses. His confidence was shaken because he irrationally moved himself from the winning category to the losing category. He simply couldn't see himself in both categories. He couldn't see the color gray.

If you are one of those competitors who defines your performance as a mark in either the win or loss column, in black-and-white terms, then it's time for you to join the gray team. As you've already been learning, tracking your performance only records outcome goals, not actual performance. It's hard to be a winner when you keep score like that.

Victories Don't Have Expiration Dates

Unlike milk, driver's licenses, and credit cards, winning and good performance do not have any expiration dates. Once you have performed well, and maybe even won a game, that good performance becomes part of your personal history. It is yours to keep forever.

If you are like most people, you probably don't have any Olympic gold medals dangling around your neck, or a Super Bowl ring on your finger. However, you do have your fair share of victories, and they are forever yours. Barry Sanders won the Heisman Trophy in 1988. Is he still a winner or did that honor somehow disappear? Bonnie Blair is a heavily-decorated Olympic speed skater. Is she still a winner or do you think her multiple gold medals mean nothing at this point?

The plaque hanging on Raquel Martinez's wall represents her win in a district gymnastics meet in 2005. You've never heard of Raquel, but she's a winner, too, even though she didn't consider herself a winner after a poor performance at a recent gymnastics meet. While dismounting from the balance beam, Raquel lost her footing and fell. She sprained her wrist and wasn't able to continue.

After a couple of weeks of feeling depressed and angry, Raquel began to explore her thinking with me. For some reason, she had decided that she must win her last performance in order to consider her career a winning one. Rather than letting her previous wins add to her confidence and overall sense of being a competitive gymnast, she had given them expiration dates.

There are a multitude of ways to symbolize winning in your life. A journal, diary, or scrapbook are all good ways to remind yourself of your victories. Your scrapbook may not be full of *Sports Illustrated* or *Wall Street Journal* articles, but it can contain personal photos, event programs, encouraging notes from family, diplomas, e-mails containing accolades, local newspaper clippings, and old practice schedules—anything that fits your definition of what it means to be successful. There's no statute of limitations on this evidence either. And you'll never find an expiration date.

What Would Your Opponent Say about You?

One indication of a true champion is the ability to respect and recognize strengths in your opponent. As a competitor, it's also good to ask yourself this question: "What would my opponent say my strengths were?" What would they say you possess that makes you a strong competitor? Do your opponents view you as a formidable challenge? Do they notice your skill, desire, or stamina? These questions can get you out of the all-or-nothing category of being a loser. They draw your attention to the attributes that make you a tough opponent. If you can identify even a single factor about you or your performance that was challenging to your opponent, then you can count yourself a winner.

When Tyrone's volleyball team lost the state championship, he fell quickly into the all-or-nothing way of thinking. The next day, he read an online interview with the coach of the opposing team. He was shocked, then relieved, to read that the coach and his players had practiced many hours and reviewed dozens of game tapes of Tyrone's team. In spite of their preparation, according to their coach, they were still wary of Tyrone's serve and the spirit of his team. Given the strengths the opposing team had identified in him, Tyrone could no longer consider himself a loser. Even the opposing team believed he had what it took to be a winner, so he started believing it too.

What Do You Say about Yourself?

The game was tied—102 all. Four seconds remained in the game. With his toe on the line, Desmond's eye focused on the spot that he wanted to hit with the basketball. He had practiced this shot thousands of times. Thoughts went through his head about what it would be like to win the game. Then he thought about what it would be like if he missed the shot. In a few momentary flashes, he recalled missing shots on the playground as a kid and replayed the taunting of teammates who called him "the bricklayer." He felt the fear in his knees, and his heart seemed to be double dribbling.

He pumped the ball three times against the parquet floor; his eyes fixed on the hoop. In the stands, the crowd was rowdy. This was a double-overtime game and they were desperate for something good to happen. While Desmond was focused on the goal, one unruly fan stood up, took his shirt off, and thrust it in the air like a pom-pom. The crowd responded to the fan — or at least his semi-nakedness — by cheering and applauding.

Still focused on the rim, Desmond heard the growing ovation from the crowd, but knew nothing about the bare-chested fan. He began to think to himself, *They believe in me. I can make this shot. I've made this shot before and I can make it again. Stay calm, breathe.* Then, swoosh.

Desmond's story demonstrates the power of positive self-talk. He didn't know the fans were cheering for someone else. He thought they believed he could make the basket. This assumption made him believe in his own ability to make the shot, and he affirmed it within himself.

Positive self-talk is a helpful psychological skill that relies on one's ability to generate an internal monologue. Many people refer to that "little voice inside" — the conscience — that helps them to handle compromising situations. That voice has the power to guide, direct, affirm, and even sabotage your actions. But a combination of positive self-talk and legitimate effort often produces very good outcomes.

When it comes to rethinking winning, positive self-talk plays a crucial role. I can't help but think about Monica, a young girl I worked with on an inpatient unit at a hospital. This slightly overweight ten-year-old had spent most of her life shuttling back and forth between divorced parents, foster care, and residential schools.

Monica wasn't very good at expressing her emotions, except for the fact that she could swear like a sailor—yes, I do realize that not all sailors swear. But her attitude was understandable. She had already experienced more rejection than anyone should.

On Halloween, the social worker on the unit brought costumes for kids in the program so they could gather treats throughout the hospital. Each kid grabbed an outfit and started to put it on. There was a cowboy wearing tennis shoes, a football player without shoulder pads, and a rock star using a Magic Marker for a microphone. Then there was Monica. She was decked out in a floor-length pink gown, a sparkly wand, and a small plastic tiara missing a few stones. She was poised, almost demure in a way that we had never seen her before. When I saw her in her outfit I said to her, "Monica, you look so nice in your costume. You're a princess!" She blinked slowly, gave her head an Audrey Hepburn turn and answered, "Yes, I know. I've never been pretty before." I'll never forget how my heart sank when she said those words. She had given away a deep secret and was too busy being "pretty" to realize that she had.

Monica's self-talk changed somewhere between the time she traded her ordinary clothes for a princess costume. She went from being obstinate and irritable to soft-spoken and kind. What Monica was telling herself—her self-talk—was critical to how she perceived herself, how she would choose to behave, and the confidence she would have around others. After that, we worked with Monica and taught her how to use positive self-talk to chase away self-doubt.

Among many of its uses, self-talk can be used by a competitor to teach a new skill, instruct herself on the next play, encourage his own ability, or calm emotions so concentration can be maintained. Positive self-talk certainly preserves integrity. Just like Monica found, the words we say to ourselves can be either positive or negative and carry a lot of power when it comes to shaping who we are. Self-talk can be used to build confidence, control concentration, and manage disappointment, envy, or revenge. Norman Vincent Peale was right. There is power in positive thinking, and most of us are capable of gaining that power.

Self-talk: Strategy or secret weapon?

It took a generation for Heisman Trophy winner Danny Wuerffel to discover how deeply ingrained his self-talk actually was. As a first-grader on a military base in Spain, Danny was gearing up to run the 100-meter dash on field day. He still recalls how badly he wanted to win and how intensely he thought about the competition in advance, probably more than an average first-grader. He began telling himself, *I am the fastest kid in my grade. I'm the fastest kid in my school. I might just be the fastest kid in all of Europe.* Danny won the blue ribbon.

In third grade, Danny was taking a test and looked at the girl's paper next to him. Once again, he heard that familiar voice that encouraged him in competition. The voice said something like, *You are too smart and too good of a kid to cheat off her paper.* The voice was loud and clear.

As a high school basketball player, Danny had to block out a hefty six-and-a-half-foot-tall center who now plays in the NFL. That same familiar internal voice echoed a recognizable refrain a week prior to the game. *Danny, you are the strongest kid. There's no one out there as strong as you.* He had a good game and his team won.

Danny confesses that he'd never thought much about his self-talk and how frequently it came into play during critical moments of competition and integrity until he and his wife, Jessica, had their son Jonah.

One morning Danny got up early and walked past Jonah's nursery on the way to the kitchen. Danny's mom was in the nursery holding the baby. As Danny walked past, he heard his mother say, "Jonah, you're such a good boy; you are so strong. Jonah, you can open your eyes, you can almost hold your head up." About fifteen minutes later, Danny walked back by the nursery and heard his mom still telling Jonah he was a good, beautiful boy. At that moment, Danny realized that the voice that he had used to instruct himself in so many ways was the voice of his mother, his father, and all those who had spoken love and truth to his heart. This realization brought Danny to tears. It was their voices that he had internalized as his own voice and that, in so many different situations, had guided his integrity and confidence.

Self-talk: Not a new concept

Former Auburn University football coach Shug Jordan said, "Remember, Goliath was a 40-point favorite over David." His comment was a reminder of the way a team's winning ability can be easily underestimated and a surprise victory occur. Small in stature, young David hit Goliath with a hurled stone and dropped him to the ground, killing him on the spot.

Can you imagine what would have happened in the David vs. Goliath battle if David's thoughts about his ability to beat Goliath had been negative? David believed he could fight Goliath successfully because—in addition to the ultimate faith that God would provide the victory—David had hunted wild animals and knew he possessed the ability to be the likely victor. David *must* have used positive self-talk to accomplish his task of slaying a nine-foot Philistine soldier. His thoughts might have included: *God is more powerful than Goliath, and is on my side. I know that I can beat this giant. I have had good aim in the past and I can have good aim now. This giant won't be able to win forever!*

Five Common Distortions about Winning

It doesn't feel good to lose. And in order to reduce the negative feelings that usually accompany losing—envy, guilt, resentment, jealousy, sadness, to name a few—sometimes people are tempted to cheat or give up.

In cognitive-behavioral therapy, psychologists often deal with distortions—irrational thought patterns—in a client's thinking. In my practice, I often work with clients who are struggling with distortions about the idea of winning and losing. I usually begin by asking whether their thoughts are accurate or not. Accurate thoughts are rational and are less likely to lead to negative feelings or behaviors. Inaccurate thoughts are irrational and often create a negative emotional state or character-eroding behaviors. Let's look at some common distortions about winning and reflect on the thinking mistakes others have made.

Distortion 1: "I must win all the time."

As you read earlier, one of the most common distortions about winning is that one *must win all of the time*. No one can do well at everything all of the time. According to the old saying, you can fool all of the people some of the time, or some of the people all of the time, but you can't fool all of the people all of the time. Eliminating words like *must, should,* and *ought* is a prerequisite for accurate thinking about your capabilities. These words are absolutes that create inaccurate feelings and can cause undue performance stress.

Winning comes and goes—and then can come again. Championships, tournaments, sales at the mall, financial ventures, and big business deals don't happen in your life every day. Slumps and streaks are like the bookends of winning. Winning would not be winning without losing from time to time. Therefore, you must look at the many smaller ways you can win rather than focusing on the sporadic nature of monumental victories.

Distortion 2: "Losing will be catastrophic."

Catastrophizing is a distortion that occurs when competitors place too much value on winning. It's taking a loss that is already unpleasant and thinking about it in an absolutely intolerable way.

I had a friend in college who catastrophized frequently. Vince wouldn't get just a paper cut—his finger was severed! He, along with other catastrophizers, exaggerated the outcome of rather insignificant events and had extreme emotional discomfort as a result.

When I meet a client who struggles with this distortion, I usually begin by asking, "What is so terrible about losing?" The competitor can then begin to identify the inaccurate thinking. People who catastrophize may think losing is terrible because they've placed great value on winning a particular game or trophy or medal. If they don't win, they somehow believe their lives are less significant or have less potential for meaning. It does sound a bit catastrophic, I agree.

But losing doesn't seem terrible at all when you compare it to truly unfortunate events or circumstances such as starvation, sexual abuse, serious vehicle accidents, or childhood cancer. For every winner, there is almost always a loser, or two, or three.

Distortion 3: "If I don't win, it's because I deserve to lose."

This distortion is known as *personalization*. The competitor often views himself as being the single cause of loss — even if he didn't influence the outcome.

Rex had submitted a business plan to his supervisor, Marcia. He had worked on it for several months. After three weeks had gone by, Marcia sent an e-mail to Rex to let him know his plan had not been accepted by senior management. She told him that he should refocus his attention on his regular duties.

Rex later learned that the business plan of another colleague had been accepted instead of his and that the company would be moving forward with it at the beginning of the fiscal year. Rex's personalizing thoughts including disparaging phrases like, *My business plan reflected my intelligence and professional abilities, which are clearly substandard.*

When Rex found out later that the company wanted to use his plan as a phase-two project he would be asked to implement and supervise, he was mortified. His personalization of intelligence and job performance seemed embarrassingly ridiculous, given the weighty responsibility he would eventually have. His thoughts about the situation were clearly inaccurate.

Distortion 4: "If I lose, people will think negatively about me."

Vanessa is a senior project manager in a business strategy company. During one of our sessions, she said she felt humiliated about the way people thought about her and her work performance. I asked her to explain her feelings further, thinking that she may be the target of a narcissistic boss or a coworker with a grudge. But Vanessa couldn't tell me of a specific example of someone saying something negative about her or a time when she received a less-than-stellar performance review. Regardless, Vanessa was convinced that her colleagues *thought* she couldn't perform her job well. She believed she was a minor-league player in a major-league operation, and everyone knew it. I asked her how she knew what thoughts other people were thinking about her. She couldn't answer. Apparently, Vanessa was a mind reader.

When it comes to bad habits in thinking, I hear about mind reading more frequently than any other habits. A common thinking error, mind reading occurs when we *think* that we know the thoughts of others. Frequently, we think that those thoughts are negatively focused on us. As a result, we may feel embarrassed, insecure, or avoid connecting with people.

But in reality, verbal communication is probably the single most important factor to consider in relationships, business, team cohesion, and so on. Anytime interactions between humans occur, communication—in some form—will probably be present. Why then do we fall victim to this notion that we can actually read minds? Can you see how inaccurate thinking can be the result? When I explain this concept to clients in my office, we actually put their mind-reading skills to the test. I tell them that I'll write down a number on a piece of paper, concentrate on it, and think only thoughts that involve that number. All they have to do is read my mind and tell me the number. Clients usually laugh, but then they give it a try. They fail miserably and so would I.

The bottom line remains: We cannot read minds. Sure, you may be in that small percentage of my clients who argue that reading body language is like reading minds. If that was true, we wouldn't be faked out on the court, guys wouldn't be nervous about asking out girls, and salespeople would know what to sell customers without spending time with them first. Reading minds and interpreting body language is not the same thing. When you think that people are thinking about *you*, they are probably thinking that you are thinking about *them*. Think about it. Mind-reading is a waste of time that can get you into trouble with yourself more quickly than you realize.

Distortion 5: "If I'm not a winner, I'm a complete loser."

We've previously discussed the predicament that an all-or-nothing philosophy of winning can cause. This is also an inaccurate way of thinking that can creep into a single thought. If we don't win a particular competition, whether in business or athletics, it doesn't mean we haven't won on some level.

Another client of mine, Randy, was going through a lengthy process of being considered for a promotion. He had worked as a software developer for the last five years. His talent and expertise allowed him to survive the technology crunch in which so many other software engineers were either laid off or demoted. In addition, Randy's closest colleague and friend was also being considered for the same promotion.

After weeks of deliberation, Randy's boss called him to her office. She informed him that he would not be receiving the promotion, but that his close friend would be promoted. Randy was angry and could have easily thought of himself as a loser. However, his boss explained that the decision was based on seniority, and Randy's colleague had been with the company two years longer. The vice president thanked him for having gone through the interview process and for his loyalty to the company. As a result of his allegiance and work performance, Randy would be receiving a 15 percent salary increase and an extra week of paid vacation.

In this situation, it would have been easy for Randy to think of himself as having failed completely. He instead focused on the aspects of winning, which included a salary increase, the gratitude of his employer, and the continuing friendship he had with his colleague. In addition, the matter of seniority was completely outside of his control. Rather than considering himself a loser, Randy found ways to win.

Even when the competition is over and you've lost, rest assured that others are still watching your character perform. Your character is on display all of the time, not just between the starting pistol and the final buzzer. You may be tempted to have sour grapes if you lose, and it may be very difficult not to respond to that annoying left-handed letter "L" brandished by fans in the stands. But remember — even then your character and integrity are still on the line.

Rethink Winning

By now I hope you are convinced that there's so much more to winning than you may have first realized. There's no arguing that gold medals, trophies, and prize money are great rewards for competitors who are tops in their field, but there are plenty of ways for those who don't take first place to experience victory too.

First, learn to reframe different scenarios so you can experience more victories. When you experience victory, you eliminate any desire to compromise character and integrity to win — because you're already winning. The Special Olympics slogan sums it up well: "Let me win. But if I cannot win, let me be brave in the attempt." For many kids — and the ancient Roman gladiators they borrowed the phrase from—winning happens when they have successfully competed with courage and determination. That's just as important as any medal.

Once you've learned to find more ways of winning by reframing your performance, you can use powerful self-talk to affirm and encourage your efforts as you move toward your goals. Develop your secret weapon just like Danny Wuerffel did. His self-talk guided him when he was preparing to compete and when he was tempted to cheat as well. Self-talk kept him focused and shored up the temptation to put character in second place.

And finally, clean up any distortions you have about yourself and winning. Distortions only get between you and eventual victory. They are inaccurate, unproductive ways of thinking, and they are going to lead you nowhere. You've got a lot of winning to do, so get out there and do it!

POSTGAME REVIEW

× Look for the positive gains in negative situations in your life.
× Think of winning in shades of gray, not in black-and-white.
× Create a victory journal or winner's scrapbook where you can keep evidence that you're a respectable competitor.
× Remember that your opponents believe you can beat them.
× Recognize and turn up the volume on your own self-talk. Keep it positive.
× Remove distortions in your thinking so you will be an accurate-thinking competitor.

Know the Psychological Pitfalls of Competition

When evil men plot, good men must plan.
Martin Luther King Jr.
Civil rights leader

On a recent flight from Palm Springs to Chicago, my wife, Carolynne, and I sat next to a man reading Martha Stout's book, *The Sociopath Next Door*. Although I didn't talk to him right then, I had heard of the book he was reading and was curious about the intensity with which he was reading it.

When the plane landed and we were beginning to gather our belongings, I asked the man if his book was interesting. "I'm really enjoying it," he said. He had picked it up at the bookstore because he was trying to learn more about his former business partner whom he believed was a sociopath.

In the brief moments before deplaning, he explained that his former business partner had engaged in some flagrant financial business deals. My new acquaintance didn't know how to untangle himself from such deceitful practices. I told the man I admired his willingness to stand up for what was right. "It must have been difficult to be associated with someone who saw success so differently,"

I commented. I then took my first shot at pitching this book to a perfect stranger. I explained that I thought character and integrity in competition are in danger of being forgotten — particularly if ethical competitors aren't actively defending their honor.

He nodded eagerly, still visibly bothered by his own corrupt associate. As we grabbed our overhead bags, he turned to me and said with sincerity, "Good luck with your book. I think there's a real need for integrity in athletics. But in business, I think you are wasting your time. There's no real place for it there. You've got to do what you can to get ahead." We locked eyes for just a millisecond, both realizing what he had just said. He had unwittingly aligned himself with his corrupt business partner. He knew it and I knew it. He tried to retract his words as the passengers filed down the aisle, but he never seemed to come up with an explanation that soothed his guilt. For me, his words were an important reminder that in competition, we need to understand the minds of both our competitors and ourselves.

To help us do that, in this chapter we'll take a look at some fundamental aspects of psychology, including moral development, ego defense mechanisms, and two types of personality disorders that incorrigible competitors often have. We'll also discuss specific ways of responding to people who don't seem to have your best interests at heart.

A Map for Moral Development

Former Harvard professor Lawrence Kohlberg developed a theory of moral development that has undoubtedly formed the foundation of thousands of college lectures worldwide. His theory includes three levels of moral reasoning, with each level including two consecutive stages that grow progressively more complex. Now, if this theory is starting to sound more like an essay question on a final exam, don't worry. We'll avoid the complexities and get right to the point: Research regarding moral reasoning is helpful in recognizing how people make decisions that involve their own integrity. Kohlberg's theory provides insight about moral development in ourselves as well as in others. As we take a quick look at these stages, we'll use the story of an athlete named Rob to illustrate the connection between moral development and competing with character.

Dr. Kohlberg named the first level of moral development the *preconventional level.* He believed that most children reason within the preconventional level, although some morally immature adults might still reason at this level too. In the first stage of the preconventional level, people make decisions based on the consequences of their immoral behavior. For example, Rob may decide not to cheat during his competition only because he is worried that he could be kicked out of the game.

During the second stage in the preconventional level, people make decisions about morality based on whether or not the decision is in *their* best interest. At this stage, Rob may decide to cheat because he desperately wants the medal, in spite of possibly being thrown out of the game. The preconventional level can be characterized by immature, egocentric reasoning; both of the stages within this level emphasize a person's self-focused experience.

Kohlberg called the second level the *conventional level.* Here is where most adults operate and make decisions. In stage one, people want the approval of others. For example, Rob may avoid cheating because he knows his coach will be extremely disappointed and because he wants to be perceived as a good person. Next, in stage two, a person focuses on the importance of following rules and order. Rob might not cheat simply because cheating is against the rules. You can see how the stages get progressively more complex in their rationales. They move from self-focused reasoning to reasoning that involves consideration of others or social expectations.

Kohlberg's last level is the *postconventional level*. The stages of this level now factor in a greater sense of ethical mutuality and reciprocity for every competitor. In stage one of this last level, Rob may decide not to cheat because he believes that everyone has the right to equal competition, even his opponents. At this stage, he realizes that cheating is immoral, and it puts others at an unfair disadvantage. The last stage of the postconventional level is the most complex. Its focus is on the universal principles of ethics — not necessarily rules. Universal principles mean that moral decisions are based on the importance of human life and other abstract values, such as justice and dignity. At this level, Rob would decide not to cheat because he understands that others may want the gold medal just as badly as he does.

If Kohlberg's theory seems complex and hard to understand, you've reached the conclusion I had hoped you would: You've come to a deeper understanding of the complexities of human thinking and decision making when it comes to character and integrity. Even if you're not a psychologist, you can at least recognize when and why making the right decision is difficult.

Thinking Pitfalls That Paralyze Performance

Every battle waged in the name of good-over-evil includes an unforgettable villain. For Samson, it was sweet-talking Delilah. For

Christians, it's greedy Judas. For Red Sox fans, it's the Yankees. In *Star Wars*, it's robe-draped Darth Vader. And yes, let's not forget Lord Voldemort, the thorn in Harry Potter's side. But sometimes the villainous thinking in our story is not done by others, but by us. We're right to watch the behavior and motives of our competitors, but sometimes it's our own thinking that unwittingly becomes a stumbling block to performance and leads to our demise. As you'll see in the following examples, thinking pitfalls can paralyze our performance. And when thinking becomes repetitive and stale, it will keep us from reaching our goal.

When temptation hits and integrity is on the line, people often give themselves permission to act in ways that oppose their values. It's easy to brush off behaviors like cheating on taxes, speeding on the freeway, or taking office supplies home for personal use. If you've ever wondered why people give themselves permission to behave poorly, you've pegged

> *Learn to say no. It will be of far more use to you than to be able to read Latin.*
> Charles Spurgeon
> Reformed Baptist preacher

the exact reason why people *need* permission in the first place. They already know what they want to do is wrong, but they want to do it anyway.

They may feel guilty, shameful, or reprehensible to some degree, so in order to get rid of such lousy feelings, they give themselves permission to do something wrong, even though they know better. In sports and in business, competitors use several defense mechanisms to reduce the negative feelings that result when character is in question. In the following pages, we'll look at some of these common defense mechanisms and how they can lead us to compromise character when we use them. Once you learn types and patterns of psychological pitfalls, you can protect your character by taking a detour around them.

Denial: What problem?

Denial is a common thinking pitfall whereby you simply don't acknowledge your behavior, motivations, or choices, let alone the effects of them. A person may deeply ignore that his or her decision lacks integrity or is exploitative.

Rachel ate very small amounts of food. She was a gymnast who had been a member of a gymnastics club most of her life. As an adolescent, her body began to change, but her eating habits stayed the same. Diet soda, salad with one tablespoon of fat-free dressing, tofu, and popcorn rounded out her daily menu. When her coach asked her to consider improving her diet, Rachel insisted that her diet was sufficient and that she was in excellent physical condition. She couldn't believe her coach would think anything was wrong with her.

Rachel was in denial. She wanted to be successful so badly that her thinking pitfall actually kept her from addressing a very real and obvious problem in her life. Rachel was convinced that her physical size equaled her success. Earlier in her career, when she was physically smaller, she had considerable success. But as normal physical development occurred, Rachel's thinking didn't grow with the rest of her. By ignoring her unhealthy eating behaviors, she created undue stress on her parents, teammates, and coaches who were distracted from their own lives. Rachel was in denial about the unhealthy eating habits that she believed would make her successful. Only after fainting at a practice and being diagnosed with an eating disorder did Rachel begin to let go of the denial, giving a growth spurt to her thinking so she could have a healthier self-perception.

Rationalization: Everybody's doing it

Rationalization is another thinking pitfall common in competition. In fact, it might be one of the most frequently used excuses for permission giving. Rationalization is the manipulation of the variables that affect the reality of a situation so it can be tolerated by an individual. In other words, we can come up with some complex ways of justifying unacceptable actions just so they can seem more acceptable.

William was a college wrestler vying for a conference championship. In order to compete in his desired weight class, he made an unhealthy choice to drastically cut back on eating. He drank lots of water, took diet pills to curb his appetite, and told others his weight was much less than what it actually was. Unlike Rachel, who was in denial about her eating problems, William knew his weight management strategies were extreme. He rationalized them anyway. He told himself that most competitive wrestlers took excessive measures to lose weight at some point in their careers. He further rationalized by telling himself that his teammates would approve of his actions—especially for an important match. William manipulated several variables in order to give himself permission to compromise his integrity to compete. The old "everybody else is doing it" excuse was alive and well for William.

Minimization: It's no big deal

Another way of giving yourself permission to compromise your values is to minimize the effects of your decision. You're not in denial, nor does it take any rationalization to make the decision. You simply tell yourself that the effects of your decision will be marginal. In the long run, you believe that no one will either care or notice what you say or how you act — including you.

In William's case, he competed in a lighter weight class. He told himself that most of the media attention focused on the heavier weight classes and that if he did win, the attention he would receive wouldn't be significant. In his thinking, it was acceptable to move forward with his weight management strategies. He minimized the effect of his decision, which allowed him to continue his diet binge.

Projection: From the inside out

Projection is another thinking pitfall that occurs when people direct an uncomfortable feeling or belief they have about themselves onto someone else. Think about the large movie projectors used in theaters. The image is inside the projector on film; then is projected onto the screen. In the same way, thoughts and feelings are inside of us, but they can be projected onto others as if they were a movie screen. Let's go back to William's story.

Amy was William's fiancée. She had been supportive of his college wrestling career. She wasn't an athlete, but she was excited to think that William might win a conference title. Amy was aware of William's weight control methods, but she didn't question him about it. In fact, on several occasions she even told him, "I think your coach wants you to do whatever it takes to make your weight class. He's been your coach the last four years, and he's got a lot invested in you. He doesn't mind if you cut some corners, because he wants to be proud of you and your performance."

The projection here is fairly obvious. Amy wanted William to do well because she had invested in him. She also liked the attention she got from his athletic performances. However, she didn't like her own feelings about William compromising his integrity and physical well-being just to win. She wanted him to win too. At some level, she knew her motives weren't healthy, but she chose to project them onto the coach.

Devious Personalities Ahead

Once you've got a better grip on your own thinking and the various pitfalls you might encounter, you can move on to understanding others. While we can change ourselves, unfortunately we can't change others. So your best strategy is to understand the types of personalities who are frequently drawn to competition and know how to respond to them if they create conflict in your life.

Competition doesn't always include truth and honesty. If you are going to compete in today's world, understanding basic psychological principles, as well as personality traits that may be evident in more devious competitors, can be helpful. Don't worry, you won't be any more paranoid after you read this section. You will simply be better prepared to stand up for yourself and your values. That's part of having a competitive edge.

One of the best defenses you have is knowledge of your enemy. You probably already know people with a few of these personality characteristics: someone who's shy, funny, pessimistic, innovative, or creative. Of course, we also know people who fall into less desirable categories: people who are manipulative, calculating, entitled, scheming, or controlling.

When enough negative personality traits cluster together in one individual, that person might be considered to have a personality

> *Toughness is
> in the soul and
> spirit, not in
> muscles.*
>
> Alex Karras
> Former NFL Detroit Lion
> and screen actor

disorder. These people usually have problems in relationships, work, or other social interactions. They may find it difficult to get along with others or be flexible if situations in life somehow change without notice to their planning. Individuals with the personality disorders we're going to discuss usually see the world only from their own experience and are unaffected by negative comments or constructive criticism others give them.

While personality disorders occur in only a small percentage of people, two such disorders are somewhat common when it comes to competition: the antisocial personality and the narcissistic personality.

The antisocial personality

You've probably heard someone say something like, "I was invited to go, but at the last minute I changed my mind because I was feeling antisocial." What that person actually meant was that she was feeling *asocial* and she just wanted to be alone. If someone is *antisocial*, they behave in a way that is contrary to traditional social norms and expectations.

The most significant characteristic of an antisocial personality is a lack of remorse. You or I would feel guilty if we cheated in a game, lied to our boss, or otherwise went against the social grain for our own benefit. The antisocial personality is not bothered by his or her actions. In fact, the antisocial personality would probably view people who are bothered by immorality as pathetic, weak, or ignorant. People who meet the criteria for an antisocial personality may have a long history of calculating, illegal behavior. They can be violent, mean, and unscrupulous in manipulative ways. If they feel badly for their behaviors, it's probably only when they're caught. Though some friendly rivalries exist in sports, nothing collegial will come from a relationship with someone who has an antisocial personality.

After working for more than a decade as a project team leader for a consulting firm, Geoff had earned the respect of his colleagues and clients. Everyone who knew him considered him to be creative, dedicated, and honest. He was a visionary with just the right amount of humility and common sense.

Another project manager who had worked with Geoff for two years asked if he would be willing to meet with him to talk about his own career development. In their meeting, he told Geoff that he was a mentor and he wanted to discuss what he perceived as weaknesses in his own job performance. He said that he wanted to learn from him. The two eventually met, and throughout the course of their meeting, the coworker appealed to Geoff's sincerity and smothered him with compliments. A humble person, Geoff was surprised that he felt so comfortable talking with him about his ideas, motivations, and personal goals. He felt like he had known this coworker much longer than he actually had.

Three weeks had passed when Geoff received an abrupt e-mail from an out-of-town client with whom he'd worked for about a year. The client was angry at Geoff because she had been told that Geoff disagreed with her company's business goals. Rather than get into an e-mail volley with emotions running high, Geoff scheduled a conference call that afternoon with his client to clarify the misunderstanding.

The client said she had received correspondence from one of Geoff's coworkers that suggested Geoff didn't agree with her company's core values and that Geoff's colleague may be a better fit as project team leader. In fact, the client explained that Geoff's coworker shared his vision for the client's firm — the exact vision Geoff had shared with him three weeks earlier. Geoff had been duped by his "friendly" colleague. He had manipulated a relationship and conversation so he could exploit Geoff's knowledge. He then took the information and tried to use it to build his own clientele and reputation. Geoff found out later this coworker had been divorced three times, had been fired from his previous job, and had never actually attained the master's degree that he claimed on his résumé. Geoff's colleague met the criteria for antisocial personality.

In hindsight, Geoff wished he had been able to detect his coworker's deceitful motives much earlier in their relationship. Fortunately for Geoff, and as far as he knew, he hadn't dealt much with people who exploited others for their own gain. Since his experience base with antisocial personality traits wasn't broad, it's no surprise that he was fooled. Yes, Geoff was a visionary who wanted to see the best in people. He didn't give up believing in others, but he did develop insight about his naive understanding of aberrant competitors.

The narcissistic personality

The second type of person you should be on guard against is the narcissistic personality. Such people look out only for themselves and would be happy if you would look out for them too. Carrying a strong sense of entitlement, they can be demanding while surprisingly insecure — but they will rarely admit their weaknesses. On one such occasion, a narcissistic woman told me she was tired of her approach to life and wanted to change. She said she had always looked down on others, expected the finest things out of life, and had no friends. Narcissists need excessive amounts of attention, admiration, and praise — frequently at the expense of someone else. They think of themselves as superior to others, believing rules don't apply to them.

I recall a clinician with whom I worked who was frequently late for meetings. The chronic tardiness alone indicated potential narcissistic traits. But when he arrived late with no apology and told everyone it was because he had been "playing golf with the bank president at the club after having lunch with the mayor," well, you can imagine what others were saying about him after he left the room.

If you interact with narcissistic personalities much, you will likely be exploited or demeaned for their gain. Antisocial and narcissistic personalities can stand independently or they can both be identified in the same person.

I enjoy collecting baseball memorabilia. My collection of baseballs signed by United States presidents Eisenhower, Ford, Nixon, Carter, Bush Sr., and Clinton is one of my favorite subcollections. Since these baseballs are hard to find, my purchases are few and far between.

One winter, while surfing some online sport auctions, I came across a baseball signed by John F. Kennedy. *There's no way I could afford to add that to my collection,* I thought. Since President Kennedy's tragic death had happened so early in his presidency, baseballs signed by him are rare — and expensive. But this particular baseball was quite affordable, and I was ecstatic. Putting common sense aside, I quickly bid on it and watched it the next few days as other bids were made. With the auction closing at midnight, I stayed up to see if my signed baseball collection was going to grow. And it did!

Two days later, I received the JFK baseball via registered mail. The auction house had given me the option of having the baseball authenticated by James Spence, a national expert whose skill and credibility is unquestioned. He's authenticated everything from million-dollar Babe Ruth memorabilia to forgeries of his own signature created by crooks to "authenticate" phony items. I immediately boxed up the ball and mailed it.

A week later, the baseball was returned with a letter from James Spence. The letter included phrases such as "irregular letter shape," "lacks spontaneity," "drawn slowly," and "sizing of letters disproportionate." The clincher was that Jim determined that the baseball itself was manufactured somewhere between 1971 and 1973—about a decade after President Kennedy was assassinated. I had purchased a fake that had no historical or collectible value. I had been exploited by someone who thought he could fly below the radar of ethics and make money at the same time—a true narcissistic maneuver.

While the auction house did give me a refund, they ignored my request to discuss the history of the fake ball and its origin. I was told that their acquisitions manager would need to call me back to discuss it, but he never did. It was like nothing had ever happened. The flavor of narcissism became even more pronounced when I began to question the auction house about the seller even more. I'll never know for sure, but I've got a hunch they both knew the signature wasn't real before they sold it.

If it hadn't been for James Spence's integrity and skill, I would have suffered a financial loss at the hands of some deliberate scheming. I thanked him again later. Had I gone with my initial suspicion, done a little more investigation, and squelched my excitement about this unbelievable presidential find, I probably would have saved myself from a narcissistic snare.

Finding Authenticity

James Spence does for a living what the rest of us should do as a general rule in relationships. He looks for evidence of authenticity and genuineness. If we learned to look for inconsistencies as closely as he does, we could spare ourselves heartache at the hands of schemers. Of course I'm sure Jim would say that it takes practice to detect a lack of authenticity; I would agree.

When Jim Spence was growing up, his father and grandfather both worked on hallowed ground — Yankee Stadium. Among the three of them, they were able to amass a first-rate collection of autographs. Mix the family hobby with a healthy dose of moral awareness, some seminary training, and churchgoing values, and you have the formula for James's success.

Jim often says, "Where there's money, there will be fraud." And he's right. It's not the decent guys, but the criminals who keep him in business.

For Spence, however, having his name on his business gives it more credibility and, perhaps even more importantly, a sense of responsibility. We should use Spence's business as a model for bolstering our own integrity. We should be willing to sign our name on the bottom line of everything we do. If we are acting responsibly and with character, then our own reputation will strengthen. You won't find many antisocial and narcissistic personalities willing to sign their names. In fact, as Christians we're not even supposed to discipline such people, but rather we are to loan them a pen if they ever decide to start changing their reputation.

Armed with a Sixth Cowboy Sense

Roy Rogers, branded as the King of the Cowboys, is an icon in American entertainment history. His shoot-'em-up movies always took aim at the bad guy in the name of honor, character, and justice. He was number one at the box office for twelve consecutive years. It's nice when good wins over evil on a regular basis.

From under his white cowboy hat, Roy Rogers's son Dusty looked me square in the eye across his wooden desk as we discussed character and integrity—the foundation of his father's life. A large painting of his father hung behind him and a collection of other Roy Rogers ephemera was scattered on shelves and in cabinets. His office is just off of the lobby at the Roy Rogers–Dale Evans Museum in Branson, Missouri.

Dusty recounted humorously how his dad dealt with bad guys offscreen, too. A businessman as well as a silver-screen hero, Roy quickly recognized unethical businesspeople. "The great thing about my dad was that he had that sixth cowboy sense. He could tell who the outlaws were. He'd say to me, 'Son, that boy wears a black hat,'" Dusty laughed. Just like in Roy's movies, bad guys wear the black hats. When we compete and when business matters are at stake, watching out for the bad guys isn't a bad idea.

So now that you're able to identify the bad guys in competition, what do you do about them? Well, maybe nothing. The phrase "choose your battles wisely" is important to remember when facing off with someone whose character is in question. They've already decided that they don't have much to lose. They've already jeopardized their integrity. If you choose to take on such a foe, the following strategies may be helpful for keeping your white hat from getting dirty.

Bring in reinforcements

If you're going to address conflict, cheating, or some other dishonesty with people who don't share your values, be ready for their deceit. They won't be thinking about accountability, so you'll have to. If a competitor tries to confront you on the spot, call a time-out until someone else — for example, a coach or a supervisor — can listen to the conversation. If you discuss a sensitive issue without having a third party to witness it, the situation may only get worse. Dishonest competitors will be willing to manipulate the situation in their favor, even after the conversation is over.

Laura played volleyball in college. She was recruited as a senior in high school to be a starter on the varsity team at her Division II school. Laura's team included several upperclassmen, including Jennifer. Jennifer was a junior who had struggled to start the previous season. She had convinced herself that she would be a fixture on the team — but she hadn't seen Laura play. After several practices, Laura moved up the ranks quickly. Jennifer spent more time on the bench watching Laura take her spot. As Jennifer's envy and anger grew, Laura heard cruel rumors from some of the other teammates. Each of them indicated they had heard it from Jennifer.

What Laura didn't realize was that such malicious deception and dishonesty could indicate antisocial personality traits. She believed the problem could be solved, so Laura boldly asked Jennifer to talk with her privately. Jennifer agreed to meet after practice in the parking lot.

Before too much was said, it became apparent that she had no intention to reconcile. Jennifer, whose jealousy was obvious, made absurd comments about Laura, reiterating the rumors she had started. The next day, the negative buzz about Laura seemed to be even worse.

Laura could have spared herself this anguish if she had asked a team captain or coach to listen to the conversation. Instead, Jennifer continued to demolish her own character by spreading gossip, and she forced Laura into a conflict she never wanted to be a part of.

Check your emotions at the door

Timing is everything. When you've decided to talk with someone who has betrayed you, make sure you are calm. If your emotions are about to explode, the results can be disastrous.

In order to control your feelings, begin by identifying them. Talk with a spouse, teammate, or trusted friend. Explore the emotions that you feel. Explain to your confidant how it feels to be unfairly criticized or the target of malfeasance. By exposing your emotions, you will be better prepared to keep them in check. You may also find that your emotions are too overwhelming to confront your nemesis at that particular time or even at all.

Paige's colleague copied her every move. If Paige made a call to recruit new clients, so did her coworker. When Paige mentioned where she was going for a lunch meeting, the colleague would arrive minutes later—feigning surprise.

What initially looked like a colleague's admiration was really a competitive quest for success. Paige's colleague desperately feared that Paige's performances would overshadow her own efforts. Those with narcissistic traits believe that image is everything and should be protected at any expense.

Paige thought she could deal with the situation on her own and hoped some girl talk could remedy the situation. At the close of the workday, Paige approached her coworker, hoping to express her feelings. But the more she talked, the more she realized how much frustration, rage, and suspicion she had been harboring. The more she spoke, the more outraged Paige became—she was unraveling emotionally. If she wanted to address the issues with her peer in hopes of resolving the situation, she would need to do it without emotion.

Remain objective

When dealing with individuals who are competitively corrupt, it's important to remember that they have probably manipulated situations or created circumstances that are false. If you stay focused on the objective pieces of the story, you will have the advantage over your competitor. Objective information could be contracts, phone messages, specific agreements, or other referencing resources. If you use phrases like, "I thought you said," "My best recollection is," or "I thought you were going to," a master manipulator will exploit the situation. If you don't remain objective, they can blame you for the problem and may try to distract you with extra information. They may attempt to get you off topic through flattery, condescension, agitation, bribery, or blame. Stay focused on the topic and keep conversations as objective as possible.

Know the Psychological Pitfalls

The kind of character you possess is reflected in your thinking and actions. Examining and understanding your own psychological process can be a difficult, even painful, task. We don't want to be like the man on the flight from Palm Springs who couldn't decipher his coworker's behavior. We want to take the difficult steps now to intercept pitfalls in our thinking so we'll avoid thoughts, feelings, and behaviors that could undermine us later.

Ever since I took that flight from Palm Springs, I've wondered how the man with the book reconciled his colleague's behaviors — and his own, for that matter. Was he really a man of integrity who was accidentally swept into questionable business practices because he couldn't see what was happening? Perhaps he was uncomfortable because he was actually a lot like his colleague. If this was the case, the pitfall of projection might have been operating. Maybe the man himself lacked character and blamed his partner instead.

The psychological ramifications of character and integrity can be complex, elusive, and difficult to figure out. But by understanding basic psychological principles, you can be better prepared to keep your own character intact.

POSTGAME REVIEW

- ✕ Clarify the reasons you behave morally.
- ✕ Avoid giving yourself permission to behave corruptly.
- ✕ Learn to identify thinking pitfalls such as denial, rationalization, minimization, and projection.
- ✕ Identify benchmark behaviors like lying, deceiving, or entitlement, which can serve as a cue for antisocial or narcissistic behaviors.
- ✕ Be willing to sign your name to everything you do.

Make Friends with Failure

*My motto was always to keep swinging. Whether I
was in a slump or feeling badly or having trouble off
the field, the only thing to do was keep swinging.*

Hank Aaron
Legendary home run–hitting king

Defeated. Crushed. Routed. Beaten. No matter how you describe
it, failure isn't pleasant. But I like what the wise preacher once said:
"Folks, I've read the end of the Book, and we win!"

You have probably noticed that our culture leaves little room
for failure. The victory circle makes the front page, but newspa-
pers rarely highlight those who come in second or third. Even rarer
would be a feature article about someone who came in fifth or sixth,
even if that person had the potential to get the job done better the
next time around.

Clients often share with me the anxiety, fear, and worry they
have about failing. They dread failure at work, in relationships, in
financial ventures, and in athletics. The anticipation of loss can be
quite difficult—even paralyzing. Have you ever met a healthy person who enjoyed failing? I haven't.

Of the many factors tempting people to compromise integrity,
fear of failure is high on the list. The measure of success is always

based on what people do right—not what they do wrong. But in every competition or corporate setting where successful performances are measured by averages and percentages, failure occurs. Batters with a .300 average have failed 70 percent of the time. (For the mathematically challenged, think of a batting average as the number of times a person hits a ball out of ten times at bat. An average of .300 means the batter hit three out of ten pitches.) At first glance, success may even look like failure.

At the beginning of the 2007 MLB season, Hank Aaron still was the all-time home run hitter with 755 lifetime dingers. Over twenty-three seasons, Aaron hit a highly regarded career average of .305. But for all his success at the plate, Hammerin' Hank had his share of failures. He struck out 1,383 times in his career. That's at least 4,149 pitches thrown to him that he failed to hit—not necessarily counting foul balls! Other legendary hitters such as Reggie Jackson, Manny Ramirez, and Dwight Evans haven't even done that well, striking out more than Aaron. Yet no one considers any of those men failures.

A Dangerous Formula

In chapter 3, we discussed the differences between outcome goals and performance goals. Remember, outcome goals are simply the final score—just a bunch of numbers when the game is over. Too many competitors allow self-worth and self-concept to be intertwined with outcome goals. You can imagine what it would be like if you always determined your value on whether you won or lost. If you lost frequently, you'd feel miserable about yourself.

Brandi was an outstanding tennis player. She had been recruited to play at a Division I school on a scholarship that would fund a degree in veterinary medicine. She was smart, both in the classroom and on the court. Her confidence was bolstered by her high school achievements — making the honor roll and remaining undefeated in tennis.

Once she got to college, however, things changed. From the outside, Brandi looked like any other struggling freshman who was adjusting to a career as a college athlete. But, on the inside, she *thought* she was failing. Brandi's course work required hours of rigorous study, which always overlapped with her practice and training schedules. She won six matches, but for some reason her backhand was not as accurate as it had been in high school, and her timing for drop shots wasn't there.

> *Show me a guy who's afraid to look bad, and I'll show you a guy you can beat every time.*
> Lou Brock
> Famed St. Louis Cardinal

Brandi dangerously measured her self-worth based on outcome goals. She aimed for an undefeated record on the court and a perfect grade point average to achieve personal satisfaction. When she didn't reach those goals, Brandi felt she had failed. She had never learned to effectively deal with failing.

Many people working in competitive settings today are guided by the same useless self-worth formula as Brandi. They allow failure to dictate dissatisfaction in their lives and, for that reason, they are more likely to compromise integrity.

Rather than being determined by a win-loss record, our integrity needs to be commingled with our love of the game, the spirit of competition, and relationships with teammates.

The Failure Mind-set

Researchers at Cornell University and the University of Toledo double-teamed on the same research project, confirming that our thinking has much to do with how we perceive winning and losing. Published in the *Journal of Personality and Social Psychology*, the research took a look at silver and bronze Olympic medalists and how happy they felt about their individual performances. Traditionally, as the article suggests, our culture tends to believe the better we perform, the better we feel about ourselves. But according to this study, that isn't the case all of the time.

Surprisingly, the bronze medal winners were happier than the silver medalists. Researchers found that *thinking* determined the level of happiness athletes experienced. Silver medalists were probably thinking about how they had missed the gold medal and the subsequent celebration and fame that would have accompanied it. The bronze medalists, on the other hand, were actually happier even though they performed worse than the silver medalists. The bronze medalists' thoughts were assumed to be focused on something more positive, like being on the medal stand, the honor of earning a medal for their country, or how disappointing it would have been to have missed out on a medal altogether. Remember this when you think about your own ways of dealing with failure, losing, and defeat. Failure is a mind-set that you can control.

Imagine a fight scene from an old Western movie where one dusty, Remington-toting cowboy says to another, "I'm going to give you one shot, so you'd better make 'er count." If the good guy gets the first shot, we're rooting for him to give it his best. We know that if he aims halfheartedly, he may be in trouble.

Competing in sports and business is no different. Halfhearted shots at success will get you halfhearted results at best. You either give it your best or you'll be facing trouble soon. You either commit to do a job well or you'll regret the consequences later. Figure skaters must be fully committed to a double lutz or they hit the ice. Ski jumpers must be committed to their stunts or face a potentially fatal crash. Sales professionals must provide stellar customer service or business will plummet. Making the decision to compete with all you've got and accept the consequences, either positive or negative, is a first-class approach.

Some competitors try to minimize a crisis before it even happens. They take only a minimal risk, hoping they can deal with minimal failure. By contrast, when you fully commit to competition, you can free yourself from the fear that holds back your performance. You can't control the outcome, but you can control your effort. Therefore, you should commit to competing at your highest level rather than committing to winning.

If you give it all you've got and still fail, you haven't lost everything. If your attempt is done honorably, you still possess courage, self-respect, and an opportunity to try again. Those are traits many competitors will never achieve.

Give Yourself Permission to Fail

Once you've committed to competing, neutralize any remaining fear of failure by actually giving yourself permission to fail. One client athlete I worked with told me he intended to win first place in his division and would accept nothing less. He didn't seem very confident, however. I think his bold declaration was his attempt to deal with failure, believing that somehow bravado would make him a fearless champion. Maybe he was going to deny that failure could occur at all. That's one strategy, but it's not very reality-based. Regardless, his proclamation backed him into a corner, and his anxiety increased. When that happens, there's very little one can do to reduce worry about a possible loss.

Clients frequently ask me what they should do about a performance problem. Maybe they make errors in games, become flooded with negative thoughts, or can't concentrate. Usually, they have already discussed the problem with teammates, coworkers, or some other trusted person and are now ready to physically do something about their problem.

> *Behind the cloud*
> *the sun is still*
> *shining.*
> Abraham Lincoln
> Sixteenth U.S. president

On occasion, I have asked an athlete to compete in a particular event with the specific objective of failing. You probably think that I've gone off the deep end. But my goal is to cause the athlete to see that fear of failure isn't nearly as strong as he or she first thought.

When Zoe was a senior exchange student in France, she played soccer competitively for the first time. She realized that it was a great way to become involved in the culture and develop a social network. Her hidden natural ability developed quickly. Because she had a true affinity for the game, she regretted that she hadn't started playing soccer when she was younger.

Zoe was accepted at a Division II university and planned to pursue a degree in elementary education. She also tried out for the women's soccer team. Even with her unyielding hustle and consistent scoring, which was continually improved by constructive feedback from her coach during her practices and games, Zoe still was terrified that her lack of experience with the game would be exposed. Zoe's obsessive thoughts forced her to train harder and longer than her teammates, and she quickly became exhausted.

After we made a thorough assessment and built a good working alliance, Zoe and I decided to test out her fear of failing. Was it as bad as she thought? We knew that her team was going to have a low-risk scrimmage game later in the week. I asked Zoe to deliberately miss a goal and intentionally perform poorly for the first twenty minutes of the game. She agreed to try the strategy without her teammates' knowledge. After the scrimmage, Zoe reported to me that she felt a sense of relief about failing because once she purposely caused it to happen, she saw how far she really was from failing. Failing in the terrible way she had always imagined was hard work — maybe nearly impossible. She laughed at her coach's description of her performance: "slow to warm up, but no big deal." Zoe actually found it challenging to perform poorly. Her ability to control failure to a greater degree gave her confidence she hadn't had before.

Block Out and Rebound

Once or twice a year, a colleague invites me to lecture in his senior psychology seminar at Harvard. In my most recent visit to the Sever Hall classroom, the crew of students was particularly interested in sport psychology. This collection of seniors included a soccer player, a hockey player, more than a couple of swimmers, and even an equestrian. We discussed a couple of clinical examples of sport psychology cases and then ventured into a discussion about performance enhancement techniques.

When it came to mental tricks and strategies, these student-athletes willingly shared what worked for them and what didn't. As our discussion progressed, we talked about the less traditional enhancement strategy of practicing errors and recovering when a performance goes wrong. Borrowing basketball terminology of "blocking out" and "rebounding," everyone agreed that good competitors know how to block out thoughts of failure and rebound after a failed performance. After failing, a good competitor must block out any negative thoughts or ruminations about the failure and then rebound by being ready to perform again immediately. In order to block out a thought, it has to be there first—but just for a moment. If you let it linger, it will start distracting you from your next performance. If you're paying attention to your game, you'll know you've made a mistake. However, a competitor's effectiveness declines when he or she stays in that negative moment, replaying an error, failure, or snafu over and over. That competitor never rebounds.

Blocking out a negative thought about failure could include various strategies, but I usually suggest my clients rebound by immediately refocusing on the next task at hand. You can use self-talk, which we discussed in chapter 4, as a constructive strategy. Self-talk can be used in a matter of seconds to block out a negative thought and refocus your attention so you can rebound. You might say something like: *Okay, so I messed up. I don't need to dwell on it. I need to refocus on the task at hand right now. Let's go.*

Visual imagery, which we'll discuss a bit later, can be another practical strategy for rebounding. You can imagine yourself making the next play successfully or the bad play that just happened being blown away in the wind—gone forever. The bottom line is this: Stop the negative thought related to failure and immediately refocus on the next opportunity you have to succeed.

Although it felt counterintuitive, when I played baseball, practicing errors and recovering from them was helpful to the team. When I coached youth baseball later in life, it made even more sense to practice dealing with the inevitability of failure. Rest assured that your competition will be practicing the fundamentals of your game, but they may not be well practiced in letting go of errors, failure, mistakes, or other performance blunders. This is another way you can gain strength over failure and develop a competitive edge. If you practice rebounding from failure, you'll have more confidence to overcome it when it happens.

Say Good-bye to Square One

Frequently I work with clients who have put considerable energy into reaching goals. They've spent long hours at the gym or on the field. They've read countless books about strategy and technique. Many people strive to be something different or do something new. And—almost predictably—on their first try, they fail. "I'm back to square one, aren't I?" they ask me. In the midst of all of their hard work, it could be tempting to give up, thinking no progress had been made at all. But I always tell them the answer is no—no one returns to square one.

Square one is an old neighborhood that can't be revisited—even if we try. It's actually the point where the decision to work on goals and competition is made. From that point forward, an athlete can invest hours in physical exercise, psychological skills training, or other strategies to improve performance. But it's important to note that all of the activities following the point of decision making were not included in square one. They were new ideas, additional training, and improved skill that occurred *after* the decision was made to pursue them. Therefore, by thinking we've gone back to square one, we discount—even eliminate—all of the work that's been put toward achieving the goal. The past doesn't equal the future.

I met Nikki, a runner from California, in the medical tent at the Boston Marathon. She, along with her husband and son, had come to Boston four days prior to the marathon to enjoy some family time and get acclimated to a different time zone. Her husband was a dedicated runner with more than fifty marathons under his belt. As a result of an unfortunate ankle injury three years prior, he no longer was able to run any long distances. Nikki decided she wanted to run for her husband. She had been on the sidelines for many years encouraging him and now wanted to start her own running career.

Nikki, like many marathoners, was driven and obsessive. She came to the medical tent late in the day after crossing the finish line. From behind tears of anger, she said she could describe her problem in two words—Heartbreak Hill. Heartbreak Hill is a legendary segment of the Boston Marathon course between miles twenty and twenty-one that ascends a grueling half mile. It's during this stretch that many runners hit the wall, when they feel as if all energy to keep going is lost. Nikki described how she had struggled to run up Heartbreak Hill. She reached the summit and saw the buildings of downtown Boston in the distance. Even with most of the course behind her and the finish within five miles, Nikki didn't have the strength to continue.

She walked most of the way from that point, jogging when she could. Her dedication to finish demonstrated she wasn't a quitter. She eventually jogged across the finish line on Boylston Street, but had bloody blisters on her feet, was dehydrated, and had a bruised ego. As a podiatrist attended to her feet, Nikki told me she was angry that she didn't finish as strong as she had wanted. She thought her training was in vain and that the expense for her family to be in Boston was too much of a financial sacrifice.

"Basically," Nikki said, "I'm back to square one. All of my effort has been for nothing."

Nikki, as you can probably tell, overlooked some important factors that weren't part of square one — that actual moment she decided to try to qualify for the Boston Marathon. Square one didn't include finishing the marathon, and she now had a medal hanging around her neck that proved she had finished. Square one didn't include the new friendships that had developed in her training groups on the West Coast. Square one didn't include the family time spent in Boston, nor the experience of having her family work as a team on her behalf. Square one didn't include the pride that her husband had knowing that she was running on his behalf. Yes, not reaching goals can be incredibly disappointing, but you never go back to square one if you fail.

Find the Common Denominator

Do you remember who won the Major League Baseball World Series in 2002? The Anaheim Angels. Who won the NCAA men's basketball playoffs in 2003? If you thought Syracuse, you're right. Let's try this one. Who won the Stanley Cup in 1997 and 1998? I'll give you a clue — it was the same team that won in 2002. If you guessed the Detroit Red Wings, you scored! But now, can you name any team that placed second to these first-place finishers? If you can, you're probably ahead of most people in the sports trivia game. If you couldn't pull up any names at all, join the stadiums and arenas full of fans who get excited in the moment of victory but don't remember the champions or the losers later on.

The common denominator winning and losing share is that both have a temporary nature. When I was a young pitcher, my father would remind me after a good outing that the next game I pitched would require all of the elements that my current success just had. A good performance would need to be done all over again. He was right. It was that same philosophy that helped my mental game when my pitching was poor. I knew I would have another opportunity to play again, and that this poor performance would pass by me. Either way you look at it, winning and losing are temporary. It's for this very reason that we shouldn't prolong any misery that accompanies failure in competition. It will be over soon enough.

Planning to Fail Takes Energy

Sometimes success or failure is decided before the competition even begins. If negative predictions abound, before you know it, you'll be telling yourself that you shouldn't even try. In your mind, you've lost the competition before you ever put on a uniform.

Prior to the Red Sox World Series win in 2004, I received a few media calls from reporters who wanted interviews with a psychologist who could talk about how sports fans deal with intense emotions and whether the curse of the Bambino was real or in fans' heads.

One interview with ESPN was supposed to focus on how Boston fans dealt with losing—to the Yankees—year after year. This media request came after Boston was behind New York by three games in the American League Championship Series. The winner would eventually play St. Louis in the World Series. It was time to play Game Four, and Boston needed to win it to stay alive.

I agreed to talk about the emotions of winning and losing in competition, but I did not want to speak about how miserable life is without a pennant—again. I was also a little unsure about talking about the outcome of a game before it was played. I'm sure the producer needed to plan ahead. But I had personally invested some late nights watching the play-offs—many of my clients had as well. None of us were ready to throw in the towel. The producer said he would call me after the game to arrange the details of the interview for the next morning.

The Red Sox beat the Yankees 6–4 in twelve innings at Fenway Park, and the game ended well after midnight. My phone didn't ring, so I called the producer of the segment who said plans had dramatically changed now that the Red Sox won. The crew that was to cover the live interview at Fenway was now headed back to New York. As in most cases with the media, the moment of excitement carries the news. I didn't hear from ESPN anymore—until the day of Game Seven, the big game between the Red Sox and the Yankees.

Game Seven would decide who would be going to the World Series. The producer called early that morning and asked again if I would be available to talk about how Boston fans would be dealing with the loss if they lost such a close series. Again, I agreed to talk about losing in sport and joked about the hard work that was going into today's story—the same story that backfired three games ago. The producer, a big baseball fan himself, said they would call again after the game. Sometime during the early afternoon, the phone rang. It was the producer again, wanting to know if I would do the interview about losing even if the *Yankees* lost.

The Red Sox won Game Seven and registered one of the greatest comebacks in sports history. This story serves as a perfect example of how predicting failure can exhaust mental energy for no reason at all. I realize a television network must plan for its responses, but for competitors, thinking about failing is inefficient and a waste of time.

We can avoid negative predictions about failure by focusing on what is happening in the present moment and the potential positive outcome that could happen if we perform at our best.

Failure Loves Company—And So Do We

You're in good company if you fail. Just consider the impressive lineup of failures. As a high school sophomore, Michael Jordan did not make the cut for his North Carolina varsity basketball team. Twelve publishing houses rejected the manuscript for J. K. Rowling's first Harry Potter book before it was eventually accepted. Prior to his success, entrepreneur Sam Walton was told by his boss at JCPenney that he didn't have what it took to be in retail. Harry Truman went to sleep thinking that he had lost a presidential election, but woke the next morning to find an unexpected trip to Washington DC on his schedule. One, two, three, or even more failures don't define who you are. Failure is going to happen to even the best of the best, so accept that as one of the rules of success.

Alex Nisetich was rejected by Columbia College his senior year in high school. Along with many of his classmates, Alex posted his college rejection letters on the Wall of Shame for everyone to see. The Wall of Shame is a centrally-located bulletin board where Lincoln-Sudbury High School seniors traditionally and openly share their college rejections with everyone. Students post their numerous rejection letters from colleges and universities so they can share in the failure process together.

"Dealing with failure publicly gives us strength and solidarity.

Posting our rejection letters also lets us feel normal," described Alex, a Tufts University–bound rugby player. Again, if you fail, you're in good company.

Alex took dealing with failure to new heights by writing a rejection letter to one of the schools that rejected him. His boldness and humor made him a star among peers and faculty. Portions of his letter even made a local newspaper. He's given me the entire letter to share with you:

March 31, 2006

Columbia College
Office of Undergraduate Admissions
212 Hamilton Hall
1130 Amsterdam Avenue
New York, NY 10027

Dear Columbia College:
I most regretfully inform you that Alexander Nisetich, myself, is unable to grace Columbia's Class of 2010 with his presence. This year Mr. Nisetich applied to nearly ten schools, and, largely due to the fact that he had never applied to college before, experienced the most difficult selection process in the history of his life. The appeal of all colleges he applied to was undeniable, but unfortunately he cannot attend them all, causing him to disappoint more than a few prestigious universities.

I would like you to know that my decision is not a reflection of my lack of confidence in your ability to accept me and succeed as a university. My experience is that most of the colleges that do not accept me are not entirely discredited, and I am confident that you will be okay even though I cannot offer myself to your class. Please understand that I cannot reconsider my decision; your rejection is final and eternal.

I appreciate your interest in Alexander Nisetich, or disinterest as it were, send my condolences, and wish you luck in finding other students.

Sincerely,
Alexander Nisetich
Executive Director
My Own Body

Get to Know Your Newest Teammate

Failure is something we are supposed to work against, not build an alliance with. Right? But what if you thought of failure as a teammate? How could that change your perspective?

As we look at the reality of competing, we can't ignore the fact that failure is a factor we must deal with. Wouldn't it make sense to know everything we could about failure and accept it for what it is?

Proverbs 27:17 says that "iron sharpens iron, so one man sharpens another." Simply put, one person can make another person better, and in the same way, failure can sharpen us if we are willing to interact with it.

Successful athletes know the importance of working well with their teammates. Remember the cliché: Your team is only as strong as its weakest member. Failure is anything but weak, and it should be considered a suitable, respected member of your team.

Let's really put a spin on this notion. If failure were an *actual person* on your team, what would you want to know about him in order to deal with him effectively? Wouldn't you want to get the best out of him? Let's create a personality profile for Failure, your newest teammate, to see whether he gives you a competitive edge.

Failure is patient

Failure stays around until the competition is over. He never takes a time-out, never loafs, never runs to the concession stand, and never arrives late. He's patient and can wait out any extra innings, double-overtime, or extra periods. Just think of those many last-second plays you've seen that won the game—Failure was there. He's tolerant and can wait for you to make a mistake, or for your opponent to take control.

So what can Failure's patience teach you about winning? Failure models endurance and persistence. As a teammate, he can remind you to avoid being overconfident, to be well prepared, to never give up, and to play hard until the game is completely over. These qualities undeniably characterize winners.

Failure is encouraging

What? Failure is encouraging? You bet. Failure compels you to do your best when you compete. If you're poorly prepared and ill-equipped to compete, it's not Failure's fault; it's yours. Before you think this psychologist is clueless, let me first agree with you that Failure won't encourage you like your coach, fans, or family will. But simply by his presence in competition, Failure suggests that you have the potential to win. As competitors, sometimes the only thing we need to boost our confidence is to hear that someone else believes we've got what it takes to win. Therefore, Failure confirms for you that you can get the job done when you compete — and that can help you think like a winner.

Failure is dependable

Each time you show up to compete, Failure will dependably stand by your side. He's there to remind you to be ready to perform any time you are called upon. He keeps everyone honest about achievement, too.

A good litmus test for whether a competition is legitimate is to determine whether your performance could have ended in failure. Remember, if you can't possibly fail, then you're probably not competing.

Many professions are associated with a scam called a vanity board. A vanity board is an entity that takes the shape of a generic-sounding organization. It entices individuals to bear the organization's credential or certification. A vanity board's pitch is that you'll be better able to compete against others in your field if you are branded by it. Of course a vanity board charges a substantial fee for reviewing your current credentials, but it's highly unlikely that you will fail the review process.

When you compete, you want Failure by your side. You want him to be there to legitimize your victory.

Failure is resilient

The concept of winning and losing has been around forever. It should be no surprise that once you're retired from playing on your team, Failure will still be around to play more seasons. Failure's resilience should remind you that losing is part of the natural ebb and flow of competition. Losing happens to all competitors in their careers.

It's like another old phrase, "Where there's smoke, there's fire." Well, where there's success, there's going to be failure, so the sooner you learn to deal with failure, the better prepared you'll be to compete. There's no reason that failure should continue to be a threat to you or your performance.

Make Friends with Failure

On her flight from France, Camille thought about every mile of the Boston Marathon. She had a life goal of completing marathons in each of the countries where her three siblings lived: England, Scotland, and the United States. Unlike her first attempt at running Boston years ago, this time she was determined to finish. Almost every mile was familiar to her because she had run them before—at least those prior to Heartbreak Hill. Like so many runners, Camille hit a wall and couldn't go on.

Although Camille failed in her first attempt, she didn't quit reaching for her goal. During the three years that had passed, Camille completed the London and Edinburgh marathons. She knew that she could go the distance. It was Heartbreak Hill in Boston that was the nemesis. As she prepared, she gave herself permission to fly to the United States as many times as necessary until she completed the race. She also recalled the topography of Heartbreak Hill and searched out additional details from a running club in Boston so she could find a similar course to practice. She made the effort to run up her own *Douloureux Colline* at least once weekly, focusing on the things that had caused her to fail during her last marathon in the United States.

Camille didn't shy away from failure. She actually embraced it, developing practice strategies based on the weaknesses in her previous performance. And at the end of the race, Camille's family who had traveled from New York watched and cheered her on as she crossed the finish line. Failure had given Camille the information and knowledge she needed to win.

Former St. Louis Cardinal standout Lou Brock said, "Show me a guy who's afraid to look bad, and I'll show you a guy you can beat every time." His quote reveals the power that failure can have over us. But once we make friends with failure, we're better positioned to improve our skills and learn our physical, emotional, and spiritual capabilities. The last three verses of Proverbs 15 offer insight into what can happen when we partner with failure for our own good.

He who listens to a life-giving rebuke will be at home among the wise. He who ignores discipline despises himself, but whoever heeds correction gains understanding. The fear of the LORD teaches a man wisdom, and humility comes before honor.

Proverbs 15:31-33

POSTGAME REVIEW

- ✗ Remember that failing doesn't mean you're a complete failure.
- ✗ Decide which goals you are willing to commit to fully, casting the fear of failure aside.
- ✗ Relieve anxiety by giving yourself permission to fail.
- ✗ Block out negative thoughts and rebound so you can be better prepared to perform again.
- ✗ Focus on performing in the present moment, not failing in the future.
- ✗ Ponder the qualities of failure and how they confirm you are a worthy competitor.

PRINCIPLE 7

Use Time to Your Advantage

*You can discover more about a person in an
hour of play than in a year of conversation.*

Plato
Philosopher

The coach yelled at the umpire for a time-out and began sauntering toward the mound. Jake knew what was on his coach's mind. Jake's catcher, Gunner, tossed down his mask and jogged to the mound for the conference.

In the previous inning, the opposing pitcher had thrown at their cleanup hitter's head, dropping all 240 pounds of him in the dust. It was payback time. The coach arrived on the mound, grabbed the ball, spit on it, and rubbed it down.

"You know the rules around here, men," he barked. "What goes around, comes around. Jake, throw three pitches to this guy. I want the first two outside and the third right at his head. We aren't playing around with these guys anymore. If he gets hurt, he gets hurt."

The coach reshaped the bill of his cap as he nodded toward Jake with a wink. He then turned on his heels back toward the dugout. For Jake, everything seemed to be happening in slow motion. No, he wasn't afraid that the hitter would charge the mound and he would be physically hurt. He was afraid of what would happen on the inside — the inside of him and all who would see his action.

What would the other team assume about his character? What would his teammates think if he didn't settle the score? What would his admiring young fans think? What about the radio commercial Jake had done promoting the Boys and Girls Club? What would his coach do if Jake didn't do what he was told? What about the Bible study he was trying to start in the clubhouse? Jake needed time to figure out how to maintain his character and integrity.

Remember the Rolling Stones classic, "Time Is on My Side"? When it comes to dealing with situations that could compromise integrity, time is on your side. Our culture holds numerous values about time, many of which are reflected in familiar quips and clichés: Haste makes waste. Time is money. Better late than never. Time flies when you're having fun. And, to quote a well-known Bob Dylan song title, "The times, they are a-changin'. "

Our culture places a great value on time — but not always in a healthy manner. Microwave ovens, fast food, on-demand television, high-speed Internet, quick weight-loss diets, get-rich-quick schemes, BlackBerries. Need I go on?

Since our culture places so much emphasis on time, we should consider how time interfaces with character and integrity. Decisions are often made quickly without considering the eventual fallout. As players in life's game, we often find it difficult to understand how time works, and because of that, we unwittingly overlook opportunities to use time to protect our integrity.

In order for time to be on your side, you must fully understand that time causes all events to pass. The very moment you read these words is now something that has happened in the past. This isn't an easy concept to understand; just ask anyone who is surprised by a hefty credit card bill at the end of the month. But time is always moving forward, causing current events to immediately become history. Understanding this phenomenon is key to using time to your advantage. Remember, that moment of decision can be far-reaching.

Take the Time to Make Logical Decisions

We've already seen several types of thinking problems that can surface when dealing with character. Research completed at Princeton, Harvard, and Carnegie Mellon universities suggests that when we are emotional rather than logical, we leap more readily to impulse decisions. What can we safely conclude from this research? If you can use logic to interrupt the emotional process of making a bad decision, you may be less apt to make a decision that compromises your character.

Kurt is a 280-pound offensive lineman who hopes to play professional football. He's only a sophomore in college but has worked out in the gym almost every day since he was in high school. He's wanted nothing more than to play football at the highest of levels. Like many athletes today, as the competition for a starting position was growing tougher, Kurt had to decide whether he would use supplements to improve his chances of playing. A wide menu of enhancers was available to Kurt: Some were offered by the athletic trainer as being approved by the athletic department physician and others were offered by teammates from "outside sources."

Kurt was fully aware of the emotion that played into his decision. He was angry because he had worked hard for the last six years and still wasn't at the weight necessary to be a highly rated professional prospect. In addition, some of his teammates made it clear that they thought he wasn't willing to do whatever it took to win for the team. After a frustrating practice of being knocked around by a couple of bigger players, another team member told Kurt he should try androstenedione instead of working so hard on the weights. "Andro" is an illegal performance enhancement drug banned by sport organizations, including the NFL. The guy offering andro to Kurt said he had enough at his apartment to get Kurt started. Full of frustration and anger, Kurt took down his phone number and told him he'd call him later that day.

> *We didn't lose the game; we just ran out of time.*
> Vince Lombardi
> Legendary NFL coach

After he got home from practice, however, Kurt had time to interrupt his frustration with logic. This was a smart response on his part. He considered how this decision could affect his future, as well as the long-term physiological effects illegal enhancers could have on his body. He knew of a couple of athletes who had developed intolerable side effects. He'd even read about players who mysteriously died at a very young age after supplementing their performance this way. Admittedly, it was difficult for him to opt out of the quick fix to performance enhancement, but logic won out over emotion and Kurt didn't call the guy about the andro.

Like a lot of competitors, Kurt found himself in a situation in which his integrity could be compromised. If negotiating these situations were easy, we would never hear about penalties and fines, game suspensions, and white-collar executives being sentenced to prison.

Of course the details of our personal lives may never make the evening news — and let's hope they don't. Whether you are a cultural icon or just the person next door, you would do well to understand that when used correctly, logic can override emotion. You won't spend extra time trying to remedy poor decisions.

Let God Be Your Timekeeper

God is the ultimate timekeeper. He's the Alpha and Omega, the beginning and the end. He knows everything about us, including when our lives began and when they will end. We wrestle with obsessive planning, coordinating, and preparing our lives in great detail, often forgetting that God has a plan. His will — His game plan for our lives — is marked by time even before we're aware of it.

Even before Red Sox Hall of Fame infielder Rico Petrocelli became a Christian, he believed that God was guiding his life. In particular, the third verse of the twenty-third Psalm, "He guides me in paths of righteousness for his name's sake" is descriptive of Rico's life experiences. Having grown up in Brooklyn, Rico knows what it's like to make a life-changing, critical decision about character and integrity. His celebrated life as a Boston baseball icon, loved by thousands of fans, almost didn't happen.

While attending Sheepshead Bay High School in 1960, Rico loved playing basketball when he wasn't on the baseball field. Just like his 22nd Street neighborhood, his social groups were ethnically and morally diverse. He had friends who were athletes and friends who were rabble-rousers. Rico's personality today is much as it was then. He can still get along with a variety of people, making each person feel connected to him in a significant way.

Rico's Brooklyn neighborhood was scattered with various shops, his school was about eight blocks away from his brownstone, and a luncheonette was within walking distance from it all. Friday and Saturday nights at the luncheonette frequently set the stage for fights, trouble, and shenanigans — in no particular order.

One Friday night at the luncheonette, one of Rico's cohorts pulled him aside and tried to coerce him into robbing a local pawnshop. He explained that the shop owner — an older man — kept large sums of cash in the register. It was sure to be an easy target. Rico admits that at the time, the consequences of robbing the pawnshop didn't seem to come into focus clearly, and he was tempted to join his friend.

Today, Rico wouldn't hesitate to turn down such an offer. His successful marketing business has allowed him to build a reputation that's unwaveringly credible. But at that time in Brooklyn, Rico got only one new pair of pants a year. Life was hard. Rico credits the Lord for guiding his path that night.

Rico remembered he had committed to a basketball game with friends back at the high school, so he told the guy with robbery on his mind that he couldn't join him.

The sure payoff for Rico came later that year when he signed his first contract to play professional baseball out of high school — an opportunity that never would have happened if Rico had gone to the pawnshop that night in Brooklyn. Unknown to Rico, his friend had used a gun during the robbery. From behind a heavy security screen, the shop owner pushed a silent alarm button. Rico, like the neighborhood acquaintance, would have gone to prison if he had taken part in the robbery.

God's game plan for Rico's life was put in place before he ever put on a Boston jersey. Rico's commitment to character allowed God's perfect timing to play out in his life.

Veteran southern gospel musician Ernie Haase also knows a little something about timing. Haase and his quartet, Signature Sound, look something like a basketball team in a zone defense on the stage, and they certainly move like it offstage, as well. But Ernie's start in Christian music wasn't as smooth as the notes he now hits with his tenor voice.

Young Ernie met with success when he was part of a fifties-style music group in southern Indiana. The group captured the attention of a local hotel owner, who approached them about singing regularly in his lounge. The gig would pay more money than what Ernie was making as a sheet metal worker, and the cash was pretty tempting.

But Ernie had already committed to use his talent only in ways that would reflect his Christian faith, so he turned down the offer to sing in the hotel lounge. Just three weeks later, however, Ernie was offered the chance to sing in a gospel quartet. This opportunity was the beginning of a career that would eventually lead him through experiences and professional success that would reach beyond that hotel lounge.

Three members of Signature Sound are from Indiana. Ernie laughs when he says they were born with basketballs in their hands. Prior to every performance, the men play intense, head-to-head basketball on any court they can find. They yell, get aggressive, and push each other around. Gospel music lore claims that Signature Sound handles the ball as well as they do harmony, so any on-comers should be ready to be serenaded with defeat.

Ernie explains that performing onstage is a lot like shooting a basketball. Whoever happens to be hot—whoever is performing well onstage—that's who gets the ball. Again, it's about timing. Ernie doesn't care about who scores the most, as long as the team wins each night they're onstage.

After watching sport legends like Larry Bird, Rick Patino, and Dean Smith, and learning from gospel music heroes like Bill Gaither and George Younce (Ernie's father-in-law), Ernie Haase knows something about team building and character. Character and competition aren't new to him, however. For quite some time, he's used character as a compass. "Character is a compass that keeps you focused on what's important—especially when no one is looking," he says.

Learn to Be Satisfied

The way we use our time to pursue life reflects our character. When we are satisfied, we don't need more. When we're not yet satisfied, we keep searching until we are exhausted. It's during times of dissatisfaction that our character and integrity are apt to be compromised the most. But satisfaction, pleasure, and contentment are all within reach and can serve to insulate us against the temptation to think that we must have more (Philippians 4:11). Your decisions—either good or bad—about what you think you want will catch up with you. Be certain of that.

I once consulted with a married couple who had substantial financial problems. Their debt was so significant that it was harming their marriage, their work, and their relationship with their daughter. They fought over who would drive the new SUV, their choice of restaurants, which island they would invade for vacation, and who was supposed to pick up the dog at the groomer.

As we talked about each of these areas of conflict, we continued to come back to a single factor—spending money. The only point that the couple did agree on was that the money coming in didn't cover the expenses going out. In spite of two solid incomes, they ended up in the red at the end of each month. The husband finally put it into words by confessing, "We just like a lifestyle that's more lavish than our combined salaries. So we put our expenses on our credit cards and deal with it later." Their combined credit card balance was more than six figures. Even so, these people were not content, and their character reflected it.

Many value-conflicting factors contributed to this couple's financial fiasco. But even more so, they lacked a critical skill necessary to protect integrity. They had never learned how decisions made now could affect their future. When they threw down the credit card on unnecessary wants, they weren't thinking about the huge bill that would come later in the month.

When we cheat to get ahead now, no one will want us on the team later. Just like this couple and their spending habits, impulsive decisions will usually lead to tremendous liabilities down the road.

Take Your Time to Respond

Another good way of using time to your advantage is to let time pass before responding to a situation that you know could compromise your integrity. Often the people who put you in such binds are making decisions based on greed, anxiety, selfishness, or fear. They want you to fix their problem or meet their needs. But the solution they want usually requires that you compromise your integrity for their gain.

Riley was a rookie on her basketball team. She respected Coach Tipton, who demanded that everyone on the team be punctual for classes, practices, team meetings, and pregame meals. Coach Tipton was known as "the Bulldog" because she would bite down hard on anyone who didn't follow her rules.

Riley was in the locker room getting ready for practice when

Hannah, a senior guard on the team, burst through the door in a frenzy. Hannah was pushy when it came to getting what she wanted. When Hannah's panic mixed with her brusqueness, she was not easy to ignore. The previous day, Hannah had overslept and missed the team's daybreak practice. As a result, she knew that Coach Tipton would punish her by making her run during the whole practice. As she entered the locker room, she saw Riley and walked directly toward her. She ordered Riley to get out a piece of paper and write a medical excuse for her, disguising her handwriting as if it were a physician's.

Hannah had put Riley into an integrity bind. Riley knew that regardless of her decision, there would now be consequences. Coach Tipton, "the Bulldog," could dismiss her from the team if she found out Riley had deceived her. Hannah could make life miserable for Riley if she refused.

Riley was smart, however. She didn't respond quickly and instead changed the subject, joked with friends, and slowly searched for a pen. Hannah finally became frustrated, sat down on the bench, and forged her own letter.

Riley gave the dilemma some time and was off the hook. If a teammate or colleague wants you to do something that lacks integrity, it's best to wait it out. If you don't do what that person wants, he or she will probably find another solution.

Decide What You Want Your Legacy to Be

The goal of this chapter hasn't been to criticize people with questionable integrity. However, we can learn from them as we make character-based decisions today. You still have time to define your legacy and win more each day of your life.

Some athletes have used integrity-eroding decisions for apparent financial gain. Take Pete Rose. In 2004, he finally admitted that he bet money on baseball, having adamantly denied it for years. As a result of his behavior many years ago, he was banned from ever being inducted into the National Baseball Hall of Fame in Cooperstown, New York. But many people wondered if Pete included his admission about gambling in professional baseball just to sell more copies of his book, *My Prison Without Bars*. Since the book's publication, Pete has also been selling autographed baseballs on his Web site. The inscription on the ball says, "I'm sorry I bet on baseball." In addition, Pete will personalize the ball for the buyer. Grand total: $350 plus shipping.

What do you want people to remember about *your* character? You have a choice. Cowgirl movie star Dale Evans used to tell her son, "Dusty, your life is the only Bible that some people will read." And for Dusty, these words still echo in his memory as a motivation to promote his parents' legacy. Yes, the Roy Rogers–Dale Evans Museum still markets its movies and cowboy memorabilia, but most importantly, it upholds the values of the late Roy Rogers and Dale Evans. Dusty hopes that when all is said and done, "it's their values that we can leave behind," because he knows how important that legacy was to his parents.

> *Sports do not build character. They reveal it.*
> Heywood Hale Broun
> Sportswriter and commentator

In 1941, after walking around the rodeo shoot at a Madison Square Garden performance, Roy Rogers came face-to-face with a toddler dressed in a cowboy outfit, topped with a white hat—just like his. It was at that moment that Roy understood the impact of his influence.

He would have a legacy. That experience led him to think about his responsibility to deliberately shape the lives of those kids who tried to emulate him. Acting on that responsibility, Roy planned ahead—and a good plan it was. He created the Roy Rogers Riders Club Rules to help others preserve their integrity and behave in a way that reflected character. Even today, some of Roy's two and a half million Riders Club members still carry their Riders Club membership cards from years ago in their wallets. The following ten rules are on the reverse of the club card that bears the member's name:

Roy Rogers Riders Club Rules

1. Be neat and clean.
2. Be courteous and polite.
3. Always obey your parents.
4. Protect the weak and help them.
5. Be brave but never take chances.
6. Study hard and learn all you can.
7. Be kind to animals and care for them.
8. Eat all your food and never waste any.
9. Love God and go to Sunday school regularly.
10. Always respect our flag and our country.

You will have a legacy too. You can either plan for it, making integrity-based decisions that can shape who you are and what others will remember about you. Or you can shoot from the hip and try to do damage control after making a series of missteps and poor decisions. Your legacy will stand the test of time—whether you like or it not—so take the time now to make it a good one.

Use Time to Your Advantage

Remember Jake, the young pitcher we met in the beginning of this chapter? As he stood on the mound, thinking about his coach's words, Jake was flooded with questions about how his decision would affect others and his future. It's tempting to make decisions based on speculation rather than focus on the truth of the moment. All too often we worry about what others will think of us or how our decisions will give us some advantage.

Jake asked himself many questions but didn't have any of the answers. He needed those answers in order to make an informed decision. Finally, Jake decided to eliminate all of the speculative questions and boil it down to the one question that he could answer: *Is hitting this batter something that reflects my character?* For this question, he had an easy answer: no.

Jake responded with integrity and acted in a way that reflected his character. Yes, he knew he would have to deal with his coach's anger for not doing as he was told. His teammates would probably give him a hard time for not hitting the batter. But he knew that the responses from his coach and teammates would be only temporary. His character would endure for his lifetime—maybe even longer.

Since you were born, time has been accessible to you. Maybe you've made good decisions about how to use it and maybe you've wasted it. We have all done that to some degree. As you consider your character and integrity in competition, remember how that same time that was there when you came into the world is the same time that will hold your legacy for generations after you're gone— long after winning and losing are forgotten.

POSTGAME REVIEW

- ✗ Before making quick decisions based on emotions, take time to inject logic into the process.
- ✗ Consider who your decisions affect the most from day to day.
- ✗ Cultivate an attitude of satisfaction and contentment so you won't be tempted to cheat to get ahead.
- ✗ When faced with a difficult decision, especially one that seems to have no good solution, take a step back and wait to see if the issue will resolve itself.
- ✗ Make decisions now that will contribute to the legacy you will leave in the future.

PERFORMANCE ENHANCEMENT STRATEGIES

The ability to concentrate and to use your time well is everything.

Lee Iacocca
Former chairman and CEO of the Chrysler Corporation

You don't have to delve into an unfathomable theological study of the New Testament to understand that as Christians, we should love the Lord with all of our heart, soul, strength, and mind. Yes, our mind. How we think and what we do with our brains reflect who we are as people of faith.

I don't believe loving God with your mind is only a simple knowledge of Him—although that's a start. Knowledge is an ongoing, dynamic process that occurs in many facets of life. The Bible gives us important descriptions of what our brains should be doing every waking hour of our day, and not just in performance.

In his letters to his good friends at the church at Philippi, Paul gave suggestions for the focus of their thoughts. Paul's God-inspired instruction still works for Christians today. In fact, many contemporary theorists and researchers couldn't help but agree that these suggestions are good for healthy thinking in general—regardless of your faith orientation.

Get your checklist ready, because here are they are: Our thoughts should be true, noble, right, pure, lovely, admirable, and excellent. Are these things the focus of your thoughts?

Take a huge jump with me from the church at Philippi to Yankee Stadium. It isn't that big of a leap to see that mental skills can work well when they have a scriptural basis. Legendary New York Yankees catcher Yogi Berra said, "Ninety percent of baseball is half mental." Yogi wasn't known for eloquence when it came to articulating his thoughts, but he was known for his athletic ability behind home plate. If you look beyond Yogi's bad math skills and poor sentence structure, you should be able to understand his main point: Athletic performance certainly relies on physical abilities, but the mind is even more important.

Psychology isn't voodoo or a smoke-and-mirrors tactic for controlling people. Rather, it's the practical study of human behavior. We can learn from it how to improve ourselves and our performance.

Now that you know the seven principles necessary to help you gain that competitive edge when you compete, you can begin to include other psychological strategies to help you perform successfully. These principles will help you to sharpen your edge, that special something that allows you to win every time you compete. Therefore, a discussion of a few basic performance enhancement strategies is in order. Some of the principles that we've already examined, like setting goals and positive self-talk, are considered performance enhancement strategies. But I would like to share a few more useful psychological tools you might find helpful. These strategies can make you a more effective and respected competitor.

The Legend of Bagger Vance, starring Will Smith and Matt Damon, is a movie about a postdepression golfer named Rannulph Junuh. Junuh was a celebrated athlete in Savannah, Georgia, before serving in World War I. When he returned from the war, he was called on by a former girlfriend to play in a significant golf match at her financially-strapped golf course. But because of the trauma and hard living he experienced during the war, Junuh was not on top of his game mentally. Bagger Vance became Junuh's mentor. He taught him how to get his swing back and at the same time regain his confidence in living life.

The movie is filled with examples of psychological strategies. Bagger admonished Junuh to reach within himself to find his authentic swing, and used positive self-talk, relaxation, and visualization to help him get his performance back on par.

You do not have to be down on your game like Junuh to use psychological skills in your own competitions. Executives, athletes, race car drivers, and pilots use them routinely — and so can you.

In order to possess such skills however, you must practice them routinely. Psychological skills can also help you to develop the confidence necessary to buttress your character. As a result, you will be able to confirm your values and ensure your integrity remains intact. Are you ready to start using your head?

Realistically Assess Your Abilities

As you think about putting performance enhancement strategies into your life, you should first learn to determine if you have the physical ability, competence, and knowledge to perform at the level you want. Senior coworkers, coaches, trainers, or trusted peers can provide useful feedback.

Rick and I worked together for several weeks. Unfortunately, when it came to implementing new psychological skills successfully, we accomplished very little. Rick was a novice runner who understood the psychological strategies we discussed and practiced in each session. He had even read several textbooks about psychological skills before calling me for his first appointment. He completed all of the tasks I had given him to work on. Rick was clearly a hard worker and desired to be a better runner.

However, as our work together continued over the next two weeks, Rick reported that the cold, dark mornings when he trained were becoming more difficult to face. He was discouraged when he didn't reach his performance goals. He began to doubt his abilities. We decided to review our sessions to see if there was something we had overlooked. The piece of information that came into question was his physical ability. Did he possess the physical skills he needed to accomplish his performance goals? He thought so. Did he understand what physical ability was needed to participate at his desired level? We had assumed that he did, but we were wrong. Rick hadn't worked with a coach since high school and hadn't formally trained in years. He was not physically ready to compete at the level he wanted.

> *A full mind is an empty bat.*
> Branch Rickey
> MLB visionary and
> Hall of Famer

We agreed that his physical ability needed to be evaluated so we would know if his psychological skills were being used efficiently. After a few discussions with a local track coach, Rick learned where his physical abilities fell short and what areas of running he needed to work on most. He didn't have to stop using psychological skills. But, because of the feedback he obtained, he was able to use them in a different way to reach more achievable goals. In Rick's case, psychological skills were helpful to him as he developed additional abilities and fine-tuned his biomechanics.

The idea of assessing abilities isn't limited to athletic performance. It applies to most every role in life where psychological skills training can bring about improvement. Some parents may want to work on relationships with their kids but don't have enough dedicated time outside of work to be successful. Small business owners want to expand their fledgling stores but may not have the skill set to make it happen. Proper assessment of time, resources, and knowledge can be extremely useful when it comes to creating and implementing a plan for improvement.

Make Psychological Skills Part of Your Routine

Once you've assessed your abilities, be ready to make mental skills training part of your life routine. Several times a year, I receive calls from athletes who want to talk about psychological skills training. They usually want an appointment as soon as possible, because they want me to teach them psychological strategies for a major competition that's just weeks or even days away. Their telephone call is often prompted by the anxiety of the impending competition. With some consistent hard work, some athletes are actually able to develop mental strategies quickly. However, it's better when people give themselves time to build psychological skills training into their regular routines. Would a marathon runner begin to run long distances only a week before a marathon? Would a power lifter begin to lift weights only a week before a meet? Psychological skills training should be a vital part of practice and preparation. To be most effective, psychological skills training should be in place several weeks, or even months, before a competition.

The major-league philosopher Aristotle said, "Patience is bitter, but its fruit is sweet." Just like any other skill you may try to develop — keyboarding, snow skiing, or balancing your checkbook — you must practice psychological skills. Practicing will take patience, but the payoff is usually worth it. By making psychological skills training part of your routine, you'll increase the effectiveness of the particular strategies you choose to use.

Visualize Your Success

You may have used visualization well before you ever realized it. As a child, you closed your eyes, made a wish, and blew out candles on your birthday cake. When you closed your eyes, perhaps you saw a red wagon, a dollhouse, a go-cart, or a pony with a brown leather saddle. (I never did picture turtlenecks, but they kept appearing year after year.) When you pictured your wish in your mind, you were using a basic form of a performance enhancement strategy called imagery. You saw in your mind's eye something that you wanted to be a reality.

Sometimes used interchangeably with the word *visualization*, imagery is effective for teaching your brain the process of a particular performance, skill, or activity. It's also helpful for gaining confidence in executing a specific behavior. When implementing imagery during psychological skills training, you should use all of the senses if possible: sight, sound, touch, smell, and taste. A hockey player might try to see the puck sliding across the ice, hear the banter of the crowd, feel the pressure of his grip on the stick, smell the slight musty odor from his helmet mixed with fresh popcorn from the concession stand, and taste the dry, plastic mouthpiece. That's imagery.

Spunky and passionate Hardy Greaves was Junuh's loyal sidekick in *The Legend of Bagger Vance*. By kerosene lamplight, Bagger taught Hardy about feeling the weight and swing of his golf club.

He told Hardy to close his eyes and keep swinging until he could see the club hit the ball.

As a twelve-year-old actor, J. Michael Moncrief played the role of Hardy Greaves. Today, Michael can still recall the long, frigid night when that scene was filmed. He tried multiple times to actually get the golf ball to go in the hole, but it never did happen—even with numerous takes. Moncrief admits he was focusing too much on his acting and not enough on the actual skill he was attempting. Looking back on that scene now, he realizes that he could have used visualization—the very skill he was trying to learn in the scene.

> *It is necessary to relax your muscles when you can. Relaxing your brain is fatal.*
>
> Stirling Moss
> British racing legend

Visualization also allows you mental controllability. Using this technique, you can create, or customize, the performance you need. For example, as she imagines herself performing a new skill, an athlete can increase or decrease the difficulty as it is being mastered. Imagery is also well-suited for responding to unusual situations because you can adjust the difficulty and uniqueness of skills you'll need to handle those situations. For example, a wide receiver can visualize catching a pass in the snow and in the rain, running full speed ahead, or falling and getting up again. Visualization is not limited to sports; it can also be helpful in business or academics.

One of my clients, Amanda, is a pharmaceutical representative. When she first entered the pharmaceutical industry, she met face-to-face with physicians and nurses to discuss the medications her company engineered and distributed. As her company downsized, she was asked to distribute information to physicians in larger groups rather than in individual meetings. The best way to manage her new assignment was through lunch presentations at local hospitals. Amanda enjoyed her speech and debate course in college, but she didn't have the confidence she wanted for speaking in front of large groups. Through visualization, however, she was able to work on her skills and imagine her success before each event.

While some people visualize their experience as though they were looking at the situation through their own eyes, others visualize as if they were watching themselves from a distance, as if they were on television. Amanda visualized her presentation through her eyes—as if she was seeing the audience in front of her. She imagined standing in front of her familiar slide presentation. She saw distinct faces of various physicians in the audience—eating and clanging their silverware while she talked. She heard hospital pages and beepers sounding. She imagined the smell of the chicken parmesan that was being served, as well as the plastic and ink odor emanating from the promotional materials and complimentary advertising pens she had brought with her. She practiced smiling, using good posture, and projecting her voice. She saw herself making good eye contact and answering questions confidently. Amanda's use of imagery helped her gain poise, reduce anxiety, and make exceptional presentations.

A college baseball coach called me about one of his players. He said the athlete was somewhat of a worrier and thought it might be helpful to talk about some strategies for managing anxiety.

When I met with the player, he began to tell me about his struggles on the field. As he described his thoughts and feelings, it became clear he was experiencing more than just a little worry. He met the criteria for an anxiety disorder and mild depression that could be traced back to the chronic dread of possible embarrassment related to his performance on the ball field. He even knew when his problem began.

As a senior in high school, he struck out during an important game with the winning run on third base. He was overwhelmed with disappointment and self-recrimination. Since that time, he couldn't hit the ball if someone was on base—any base. We talked about different options for conquering this mental block, including imagery. The athlete wanted to pursue this option because he believed that if he could go back in time and hit the ball, the problem he was having today would disappear forever. And he was right.

He visualized himself hitting various types of difficult pitches with runners on the bases. He visualized hitting a curveball with runners on first and third. Then, he visualized hitting a slider with a man on second. After three sessions where we used imagery, followed by the athlete regularly practicing at home, the hitter was able to return to a consistent batting performance and was free of anxiety or embarrassment.

Associate with Success

Association and dissociation are two thinking strategies often used in sport and exercise psychology. *Association* occurs when a person is focused on his or her own internal physical process as it occurs. A physical process could include many sensations like a heartbeat, breathing, muscle tension, or a runner's high. Often, an athlete can pair his or her internal experience with an image. A marathon runner gave me a good example of associative thinking when he described the following to me:

"Sometimes when I'm so tired from running, I can't feel my legs," he observed. "I know they are working because I'm moving forward, but that's about it. I don't want to quit, so I start thinking my legs are moving with the same force and intention as a locomotive striding up a mountainside. I can start feeling my legs again as I chug, chug, chug, chug in the same pattern that I see the engine moving along."

This runner remained well aware of his internal physical and emotional experience by keeping his attention focused on important physical performance cues. He used imagery to help maintain his focus and performance—even when he was fatigued.

Another clever way of using association is to derive strength from a favorite person, hero, or mentor. Many Bostonians would say that former Red Sox hero-turned-villain Johnny Damon would have been their go-to man for making good decisions. At one point in Red Sox history, a fan could even find several versions of T-shirts bearing the question "WWJDD?" With his long hair and beard, many people thought Damon had the likeness of Jesus. Indeed, whether it is "WWJD" or "WWJDD," such paraphernalia serves as a good reminder that people in our society are still willing to have role models powerfully influence their lives.

Whether you look to Jesus or Johnny Damon (hopefully, for Christians, Jesus is the standard), asking yourself what your role model would likely do in a particular situation is a good strategy for making tough decisions that can affect your integrity. Using the strategy of association, you will be able to notice your internal experience and then ask yourself this question. "What would _____ do in this situation?"

Former U.S. Attorney General John Ashcroft tells several stories in his book *Lessons from a Father to His Son*, about how he frequently looked to his father's character and integrity as he faced the responsibilities of politics and daily living. Ashcroft filled the blank with his father's name.

Dissociate When Necessary

Dissociation is used when attention is drawn away from internal physical performance cues and is placed on external stimuli. Unlike the debilitating type of dissociation that is a symptom of post-traumatic stress disorder, this type of dissociation is an intentional phenomenon. It might also be referred to as distraction.

Let me preface this section with this warning: While some research correctly suggests dissociation is a potentially more effective strategy for managing performance pain, it also comes with a greater risk for injury. Ignoring any messages that your body sends to you about pain could be detrimental to your health. Dissociation used for minimizing pain should be used cautiously.

A runner I met after the marathon told me how she used dissociation to manage her performance. Instead of focusing on the internal cues created by a blister on her foot, she chose to focus on the buildings she passed, the people she saw, and the blue sky above her. These detailed images distracted her from her pain and made it temporarily manageable. Dissociation means to distract—not ignore. Your safety and health should never be compromised in the name of a performance.

Map Your Success

A precompetition routine is a pattern or sequence of activities that you can use before competition. As a performance enhancement strategy, a precompetition routine serves many purposes. It can reduce performance anxiety, increase focus and concentration, or manage other factors that are part of your performance.

Such a routine also allows you to have consistency in your performance and preparation, which will ultimately guide you toward the performance goals you've set. It helps you focus on the task at hand, while blocking out other interfering factors.

You can think of a precompetition routine like you would an assembly manual. Step one is followed by step two and then those pieces are put together for step three. It consistently guides the performer, step-by-step, toward the finished product which, in our case, is a good performance. It's helpful for preparation to be consistent every time you compete. It's not uncommon for a precompetition routine to begin the morning of a competition and lead up to the time performance occurs.

A few years ago, I met with Kristine, a single woman who worked as a commercial real estate broker. The commercial real estate business is demanding, requiring many miles of travel and stamina. Throughout the course of her week, Kristine conducted business in all four time zones in the continental United States. She developed a precompetition routine as a way of managing her travel stress, dealing with fatigue, and staying focused in meetings. She always traveled with the same airline, rented from the same car rental company, and alternated staying in her two favorite hotels. Her travel schedule was physically and emotionally demanding, but she enjoyed much of her work. She tried to schedule her arrival in each city so she would still have telephone time with friends and family. She allowed time to eat a meal in her hotel room as a way of feeling like she was home. She made room in her schedule to exercise in the morning and have a good breakfast.

Memorizing your routine in checklist form can be helpful, as can developing an acronym or symbol that reminds you of the specific order of your performance. Every time Kristine traveled, she used the acronym THIEF. Travel, Hotel, Important people to call, Exercise, and Finally go to bed. She often said she was going to be a THIEF and steal back all of the things that her busy job robbed her of.

Each of these steps allowed Kristine the opportunity to focus on her job. Most of us won't have to travel extensively like Kristine — and she didn't do it forever. But we do need to focus on our work and manage factors that are outside of our control the best we can. Using a precompetition routine provides a sense of control and predictability that can lead to better job performance.

An internationally competitive sailor with whom I consulted agreed to let me share his precompetition routine with you. The routine is both cognitively and physically detailed, and it is printed on the front and back of a single page. Ready for practice or race day, he kept his routine in a clear plastic bag in his frequently wave-dowsed boat. His detailed routine focuses on starting his performance when he rises in the morning. The routine unfolds to include specific preparation for sailing, allowing for changes in race conditions, developing strategies, warming up, and timing the start.

PRERACE ROUTINE

Shore and Water

AT HOME:
- ✓ Get up at 6 a.m.
- ✓ Shower.
- ✓ Dress in usual comfortable clothes.

✓ Pack sailing gear and change of clothes.
1. watch
2. hat
3. life jacket
4. boots
5. dry underwear
✓ Eat traditional breakfast food.
✓ Take an hour of "down time" by reading paper, watching television.
✓ Have one cup of coffee.
✓ Apply sun block and clean sunglasses.
✓ Load car with gear.

AT THE CLUB:
✓ Walk around the venue and docks with coffee, visit with others.
✓ Find the boat and start getting it ready:
1. Take covers off the boat.
2. Check all lines and fittings for wear and any problems.
3. Sponge out water.
4. Untwist any lines, including mainsheet.
5. Put gear, food, and water in boat.
6. Raise the jib, and check rake and tension.
7. Put boat in the water, and leave bridal on shore.
8. Tie boat off.
✓ Go to the bathroom.
✓ Begin mental focus time: Clear my mind and use visualization to get rid of distractions.
1. Find a quiet place for visualization.
2. Visualize distractions written in the sand and then let the wind blow them away.
3. Visualize navigating a tight racing situation, mistake, or bad break successfully.

ON THE WATER:
- ✓ Be on the race course twenty minutes before the first gun.
- ✓ Check in with the race committee.
- ✓ Take a wind shot on or near the starting line.
- ✓ Sail upwind on starboard and port sides. Record compass headings.
- ✓ Visualize: "If we were starting now, which way would we go based on what I see now?"
- ✓ Do five tacks in quick succession. Turn downwind, launch pole, and be set up for a run.
- ✓ Do five jibes in quick succession. Determine if tide or current are factors. Determine if, when, and how they may change.
- ✓ When the starting line is set, do a wind shot and then run the line to determine favored side of course.
- ✓ At the five-minute gun, develop a final game plan by answering these questions with self-talk:

Where do we start and why?

What is the likely first shift?

Which side looks favored?

**What will likely be the best
approach at the weather mark?**

- ✓ At the four-minute gun, do another wind shot and look up the course.
- ✓ Ask the question: Is there a change that seems to be an

oscillation or persistent? If yes, how is the game plan affected?

✓ At two minutes, take a final look up the course and ask the same questions.

✓ At one minute, maintain observations, changing game plan quickly only with good reason.

✓ Execute the game plan!

If you use a precompetition routine as a performance strategy, it's important to keep it somewhat flexible. If a routine becomes too rigid, there will be no room for adjusting strategies or techniques without feeling anxiety or guilt.

A precompetition routine should be about planning and preparation, not superstition. For example, if your routine included a pasta meal and pasta wasn't available, you'd need to be flexible enough to eat a different type of meal. Something bad is not going to happen just because you don't eat pasta. You need to focus on the fact that eating is a part of your routine, and then stay on track with that part of your routine. Rigidity with a precompetition routine can lead to unwanted anxiety, defeating its entire purpose.

Relax Your Body and Mind

Maybe you've been there. You were in a game, struggling to do your best. Your coach or teammates, or maybe your parents or rowdy fans, yelled those dreaded words of encouragement: "Just relax!" If relaxing in a tough situation were only that simple, you would have already done it. Any type of performance can be stressful. Whether you're preparing for a big game or business meeting or managing a hectic household, stress can positively or negatively affect performance. Even Scripture recognizes that we need to be still and relaxed (Psalm 46:10).

When included in a competitor's psychological skills toolbox, relaxation can be used to manage stress or emotion before or during an actual performance – or any time life calls for calm composure. Since relaxation can occur in several different forms, it is usually accessible in many performance situations. For some competitors, relaxation can easily be evoked by visualizing a special place or a meaningful word that signals a relaxation response in the competitor.

Some competitors find that controlling breathing during stressful times is an effective way of relaxing. One deep cleansing breath is helpful for some, while more patterned, paced breathing is helpful for others. Nevertheless, some competitors *hold* their breath, which will likely contribute to a negative performance. Breathing is a natural part of our body's function, just like muscle exertion and thinking. Unless you are a water-sport athlete, holding your breath can be a sign of anxiety or lack of confidence.

Other competitors may choose to use a more traditional form of relaxation called progressive muscle relaxation. Progressive muscle relaxation, also called the Jacobsonian relaxation technique, can be used before or following a competition or performance. This technique is simply an organized pattern of tensing and relaxing muscles throughout the body. You begin with a single group of muscles such as your feet, then move on to your calf muscles, then quadriceps, and so on until you have included all of the main muscle groups in your body. Many athletes, as well as others in high performance situations, report this strategy to be effective for reducing stress and anxiety related to tension and performance.

Go. Now. Smooth. Blue. Energy. Easy. Calm. Cue words are

special or unique words that an individual uses to bring about a preferred state of mind before, during, or after a performance. Useful in many ways, cue words can be used to initiate activity or energy, calm nervousness through relaxation, or increase focus.

In my desk drawer is a signed picture of a power lifter I worked with several years ago. He used the cue word "now" when he was ready for a weighty bench press, dead lift, or squat. For his bench press, he would lie on the weight bench, hands lightly grasping the bar. At the end of a long, deep breath, he said the word "now" in his mind. At that point, all of his energy, focus, and strength went into his performance—and he would lift. For this athlete, using a cue word was a useful strategy for bench pressing over 350 pounds in a national competition where he claimed first place.

A former client of mine worked for a cosmetics firm. She had an employee evaluation every quarter. She disliked being scrutinized by her supervisor, and even became nauseous prior to her evaluation meeting. Once in the meeting, she reported feeling overwhelmed and light-headed, which caused her to make some very silly comments. Over time, however, she learned to use a cue word to help regulate her nervousness. She chose the word "breeze." For her, "breeze" had several meanings. First, she wanted to remind herself that each of her prior evaluations had been a breeze and this one would be a breeze, too. She also liked the word *breeze* as a cue word because it helped her remember the breeze she much enjoyed as a kid when playing at the beach on Cape Cod.

While verbal cues are useful in prompting a certain psychological response, physical or psychomotor cues can also be used. Clever examples include patting a leg, taking a deep breath, running a hand through one's hair, or adjusting a piece of a uniform. The options for psychomotor cues are limitless and can be easily tailored to the athlete and sport in such a way that no one watching would ever know you are using them.

I consulted with a college basketball player who described the anxiety she felt during exams. She also admitted feeling the same way during basketball games, especially right before she made a three-point shot. Her teammates would have been quite surprised to know this, since she was an excellent shooter and never displayed any anxiety.

We discussed the fact that psychomotor cues could be helpful in prompting her to relax. We used progressive muscle relaxation over the course of the next two sessions. She also practiced relaxation daily in her dorm room. After mastering relaxation rather quickly, we paired a psychomotor cue with the relaxation. She decided her physical cue would be two heartbeat pats on her leg. Thump, thump. Thump, thump. She chose the heartbeat pattern because it represented a steady, relaxed pace rather than a racing, anxious heartbeat. These techniques allowed my client to relax in any situation, and then to succeed.

The Final Outcome

Yogi Berra is known for saying, "It ain't over 'til it's over." Well, this book *is* about over, but the daily situations that will challenge you to win will continue far beyond these pages.

You've now introduced seven new principles into your life, which give you the competitive edge you'll need to win every time you compete. These principles will give you a firm foundation on which to stand, allow you to tighten your grip on values, and increase your confidence as you battle for what is right. If you need to, write down these seven principles and put them someplace where you'll find them easily. They're yours to keep forever. Here they are one more time:

Know the rules of the game. Second Timothy 2:15 encourages study, knowledge, and the pursuit of truth. In all aspects of your life, you should strive for increasing knowledge of who you are as a competitor and about the game you are playing. The rules of a game can change. Therefore, know them well so you can't be duped. Knowledge is power, and power brings about strength, determination, and stamina for winners.

Recognize the right decision and make it. Don't be surprised when you face tough decisions. If you aren't challenged daily, you probably aren't really in the game. Decisions are a fact of life, and you've got to make them decisively so your character and integrity aren't lost in ambiguity. Making decisions that reflect your values will not only help you win the battle, but guarantee that you'll win the war.

Define goals that reflect your values. You must clearly and accurately identify the target you are aiming for. If you take aim at goals that reflect less than your values, you'll surely hit them. Fix your eyes on goals that reflect your character and integrity, and never become distracted by less honorable endeavors.

Rethink winning. Christians aren't supposed to be conformed to the world. Therefore, we have the opportunity to rethink what winning really is each time we compete. If you keep your integrity intact, yet fall short of the grand prize, you will still be a winner.

Know the psychological pitfalls of competition. Even knights have chinks in their armor. As competitors who are interested in victory, we must understand the weaknesses and pressure points that make us vulnerable to compromise. Once we recognize them in ourselves, we'll be able to recognize them in our rivals as well. You must think like a winner.

Make friends with failure. The best way to negotiate failure is to eliminate its power. By understanding that failure, like winning, is a natural part of competition, it can actually confirm you are a worthy competitor. You deserve to be in the game. When you neutralize failure's power, you'll have a fearless command over it and be in a position to win in the middle of loss.

Use time to your advantage. Time is multidimensional. It's like a stealth bomber that sneaks up on you. Time represents the number of days you live, and it will be used to characterize your life after it is over. When you're gone from this earth, people will talk about the good times they had with you and what you spent your time doing. Time also reminds us of the importance of decisions. Take time, now, to sharpen your competitive edge.

So now it's time for you to use your competitive edge to advance toward the victory. Believers are encouraged to press on toward the goal to win the prize for which God has called us in Christ Jesus (Philippians 3:14). Your team is counting on you, so run hard for a strong race. It will be at the finish line where your Coach, your heavenly chief executive officer, will greet you. He'll welcome you into *The* Hall of Fame and present to you the trophy of all trophies, inscribed with the words, "Well done, good and faithful servant." That will be the finest victory ever.

AFTERWORD

Everyone in our house knows that after a bad outing on the mound, the next few days can be pretty miserable for me. After one particularly bad night I was riding home with my son Gehrig and the car was silent as usual. Gehrig looked at me and said, "You okay, Dad?"

"Yeah, just disappointed in how the night went," I said.

"Dad, you always told me that if I do everything I can to be my best, that is all that matters, regardless of the outcome."

The Lord works in mysterious ways. Thirty minutes after a game ends — a game in which fifty thousand people in the ballpark watch me have a horrible night — my eleven-year-old son breaks out that pearl of wisdom and ends any chance I have of feeling bad or sorry for myself.

Even more exciting is the thought that my oldest son truly gets it. At an age when there are a million stressful things going through his mind, from grades to peer pressure, he calmly reassures me, his dad, that everything's going to be okay.

You see, regardless of who you are or what you do, you have plenty of opportunities to make decisions about doing what is right. Whether on the job, in school, on your team, in the public eye, in the privacy of your home, or with friends, family, or strangers, the way your integrity shows through to others is up to you. Sometimes doing the *right thing* isn't popular, but it still needs to be done.

My wife, Shonda, and I tend to be very passionate about things

159

in life that matter to us most, but we'll be the first to admit we sometimes make poor decisions, say the wrong things, have bad timing, and act on emotion rather than common sense. Of course, admitting our faults doesn't excuse us from the responsibility of cultivating integrity on a daily basis. But when we screw up, God is there to clean up the messes and reshape our lives to better reflect Him to others. The Schilling family knows that even when we lose on the outside, we can still win on the inside. That's what matters most.

I've played professional baseball for nearly two decades and have been challenged by some of the best hitters to ever swing a bat. A few years ago, my character was put in the spotlight when I was subpoenaed to testify before the House Government Reform Committee about steroid use in baseball. I chose to stand on integrity, be honest, and make myself available to help solve this problem in whatever way I could.

Believe me, you don't have to play baseball for championship teams like the Boston Red Sox or Arizona Diamondbacks for your integrity to be tested. As a couple, Shonda and I have faced our fair share of stiff competition in our personal lives as well. In 2001, Shonda was diagnosed with skin cancer. She battled melanoma and eventually won. Recently, she ran her third Boston Marathon to raise money for the SHADE Foundation, an organization which she founded as a way of educating others and preventing skin cancer. She works hard so others can have victory over skin cancer too.

As a family, we have carried every banner we can lift on behalf of the ALS Association. You've probably heard of ALS—Lou Gehrig's Disease. We're not just spokespeople on behalf of the association, but we've lived our lives interacting and intertwined with victims of ALS. During Shonda's struggle with melanoma, many ALS families reached out to her because of the relationships we've shared. Many of them carried our banner for a while and for that we are tremendously grateful.

We can't always choose our battles, but we can be geared up to fight them when they come. Our faith and values seem to have always gotten us through when winning on the inside was the priority.

We've learned that when it's all said and done, our character and integrity are the only things that remain. At the end of life's journey there may be a few reminders of where we've been—a couple of World Series rings, a bloody sock, and used marathon bibs to name a few. But for us, a life well lived goes much deeper and reaches much further than those souvenirs. Life is about deepening relationships with teammates and families. It's about extending lives of ALS patients. It's about avoiding skin cancer and implementing laws about sun exposure awareness. It's about living our personal lives within earshot of the media and still standing upon principle—even when it gets complicated. It's about raising our kids in a way that they will want to give to others too.

Like Gehrig reminded me: It's going to be okay as long as you do the *right thing*. Let's be honest, though. Doing the right thing isn't easy in today's world. Everywhere we look, we see people competing for what they think will make them happy: money, fame, power, and the list goes on. Remember, as Christians we aren't supposed to be conformed to what the world says we should be. We need to compete in a different way and that's why we need to develop a competitive edge to win when it matters most.

We agree with Dr. Brown's assessment that people need to have a way of protecting their character in our society. Like him, we want people to be able to win every time they compete—without losing character and integrity in the heat of the moment. Jeff's understanding of how people think and behave, combined with his insight into competition in sport, business, and life, will help you invest in something far greater than you could imagine. We want you to have the competitive edge too.

God bless you and yours,

Curt Schilling

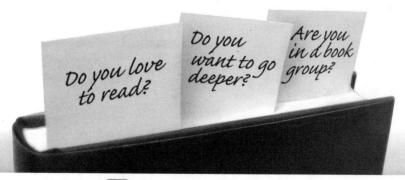

Every day you're faced with choices that will impact your future.

What choice will you make today?

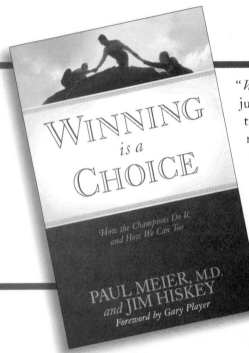

"*Winning is a Choice* is not just for the athlete. It's for the teenager, housewife, teacher, mentor, businessman, or stateswoman. Give this book to someone you love or someone facing adversity and it may well become one of the greatest books they'll ever possess."

Gary Player, pro golfer

Through the inspiring stories of real-life champions, including famous figures such as Tiger Woods and Lance Armstrong as well as everyday people, golf pro Jim Hiskey and well-known psychiatrist Paul Meier outline the eight critical choices that champions face, and demonstrate that the real winners are individuals who make wise decisions when confronted with adversity.

FOREWORD BY *Steve Forbes* | AFTERWORD BY *Zig Ziglar*

HIGH-PERFORMANCE ETHICS

10 Timeless Principles for Next-Generation Leadership

WES CANTRELL
JAMES R. LUCAS

Want to follow the 21st-century path to success?

Wes Cantrell, a highly respected and well-known business executive, has seen success and strong values go hand in hand throughout his nearly fifty-year career. In *High-Performance Ethics*, he teams up with James R. Lucas, an internationally recognized leadership consultant, to reveal a truly surprising secret: The road of principle is also the road to higher performance and richer results.

In this book, the authors set forth ten timeless principles of ethical, results-oriented leadership and teach you to apply them to the high-paced, high-stakes world that next-generation leaders like you are facing right now.

LEADERSHIP ABOVE THE LINE

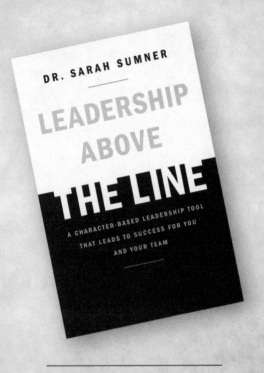

If you're working "above the line," you're in your unique success zone—leading with excellence and character in the way that best fits your strengths. *Leadership above the Line* uses Jesus as the model of the ideal balanced leader. Dr. Sarah Sumner offers practical tools to help you incorporate above-the-line strengths into your everyday life. Available everywhere books are sold.